DATE DUE

| | | | |
|---|---|---|---|
| JAN 24 | | | |
| OCT 27 | | | |
| FEB 21 | | | |
| OCT 5 | | | |
| | | | |
| | | | |
| | | | |
| | | | |
| | | | |
| | | | |
| | | | |
| | | | |

# THE MEANING OF MODERN ATHEISM

*Jean Lacroix*

*Translated and introduced by*
GARRET BARDEN, S.J.


THE MACMILLAN COMPANY
NEW YORK
1965

*First published* 1965





*Originally published as*
LE SENS DE L'ATHÉISME MODERNE
*by Editions Casterman, Tournai*

*Library of Congress Catalogue Card Number* 65–22610



Nihil Obstat: EDUARDUS GALLEN,
*Censor Theol. Deput.*

Imprimi Potest: ✠JOANNES CAROLUS,
*Archiep. Dublinen,*
*Hiberniae Primas.*

*Dublini, die* 7° *Maii, Anno* 1965.

Printed in the Republic of Ireland

CONTENTS

# Introduction

It is not the purpose of the essays collected here to show that atheism is false. The reader must not expect to find a refutation of atheistic thinking. The author's aim is to understand, not to disprove. For too long Christians have been content to dismiss opposing points of view as erroneous and futile, while making little attempt to understand why these opinions were held. Yet if the Christian truth is to be brought to all men, the Catholic Church, in the words of Pope Paul VI, must look beyond the confines of the Christian horizon. And she must look not with censure but with understanding. Throughout the Second Vatican Council there has steadily grown the recognition of this responsibility.

It is not true that the Christian message is irrelevant in our day. Still, it is true that it has not seemed relevant. To many Christianity and the Church have appeared anachronistic. At best the Church is a once important institution which has outlived its usefulness, or at worst the remnant of an ancient and oppressive superstition. For Sir Julian Huxley, to take a writer with whose name many readers will be familiar, the idea of a God is a stage in an evolutionary process. Today that stage is past, and 'we must melt down the gods and refashion the material into new and more effective organs of thought'. The material mentioned is the experience of the holy described by R. Otto and taken up by C. G. Jung who identifies it with the archetype 'self'. The gods are no more than projective images of this basic numinous experience. The gods are symbols which must not be allowed to claim any other mode of existence than the symbolic. When the gods—and for Huxley the Christian God is one of the vast array of gods and no more than this—are allowed objective existence, then superstition reigns; and therefore to obviate this danger of the symbols becoming real a 'humanist religion will have to work out its own rituals and its own basic symbolism'. For this kind of atheism Christianity is an outworn form in the evolutionary development, and the Church is the enduring bearer of superstition. It would be interesting to delve into the nature of this kind of atheism, but space forbids. Because it has stressed the non-rational elements in the experience of the holy and the universal need for symbolism on an emotive level, it might throw some light on the nature and function of liturgy and ritual in the modern world.

Humanist religion, however, is neither the only nor the most widespread form of atheism. Humanist religion stresses man's symbolic nature; the forms of atheism examined by Lacroix have as common factor the insistence on human responsibility. Lacroix shows the relation that is thought to exist between human responsibility and the denial of God. Why is the acceptance of God's existence thought to be a denial or at the very least a serious curtailment of man's personal responsibility? There are many reasons. One of them may be that, as Michael Novak puts it in the introduction to *The Open Church*,[1] 'for centuries the Church has not *appeared* to be developing a Godlike race. It has not appeared to be forming men to integrity, to courage, to humble charity. It has seemed to many to call men to lead an unreal life, an irrelevant life.' Maybe because of this many drift away from the Church and from God. Too often the Christian is one who has appeared to have abdicated from the sufferings and responsibilities of this passing life.

Sometimes atheists are presented as those who have forsaken belief in God because God was too demanding. It is very salutary to read of those who have thrown off God because belief in God made life too easy. Responsibility is the key to this kind of atheism. Lacroix examines what this responsibility entails, how the fundamental conviction of man's responsibility in the world is developed both

[1] London and New York, 1964.

in inter-personal relations and in the wider spheres of economics and politics. The non-existence of God is not, for most of the streams of atheistic thought examined in this book, the conclusion of an argument. Rather is it the starting-point of the development of a way of life. For the stress in modern atheism is not on the non-existence of God but on the responsibility of man.

If in modern atheistic thought the existence of God is incompatible with human responsibility, so also is the notion of original sin. In the second essay, 'Sinless Morality', Lacroix examines this contention as he finds it set out in Hesnard's *Morale Sans Péché*. As Hesnard understands it, original sin deprives man of responsibility since it places him in a context of inevitable failure. Paradoxically a man is not guilty because he was born guilty. But if this original guilt or 'sin of existence' is removed, then a man can become guilty because he is responsible. Further, his guilt is related to his own activity and not to his very existence. Here again Lacroix is concerned with interpretation rather than refutation. It is true that he mentions that Hesnard's interpretation of the Catholic doctrine on sin is inadequate; but his main purpose is to show what Hesnard's interpretation is. For Hesnard's interpretation is common enough; and it is of great value to know how others understand sin in order that we may be goaded into deepening our own understanding of what Saint Paul refers to as the mystery of iniquity.

It is a constant temptation to Catholics to think, or at least to act, as if they were in possession of the whole truth about everything. It is the task of each Christian to develop in understanding of the dogmas of the Church, to grow in the understanding of the faith. A perfect understanding cannot be reached, but we can continually grow in understanding. This is clear enough in the individual; it is obvious that the adult is capable of greater understanding than the child. But the same is true of the Church. There is development in understanding. For instance, in the present Council we are moving towards a deeper understanding of the role of the Church in the world. There emerges a more accurate grasp of what Christian responsibility means today.

In the closing paragraphs of the first essay Lacroix remarks that Christians must show atheists that the stress on human responsibility is not incompatible with faith. How is this to be done? Not by argument, he suggests, at least not by argument alone, but by action. Christians must show forth these values in their lives.

It is easy to shirk responsibility. One can evade it by going through life unreflecting, without considering the demands that one's situation makes, by constantly dodging the approaches to self-knowledge in which the sense of responsibility would emerge. Or one can pretend that one is already perfect, or attempt to rationalize one's way out of responsibility. Or finally one can give up the struggle and remain content to be no worse than the majority of men.

None of these ways of avoiding responsibility is specifically Christian or even theist. Nor indeed can it be claimed that Christianity encourages irresponsibility. What is it then that led some to think that being a believer tended to make one less aware of one's responsibilities as a man? I have already quoted Novak who gives what might be termed the historical argument, namely that the Church does not seem to be forming men to integrity. But why is this the case? Is it that the admission of an after-life diminishes one's responsibility in this one? Certainly, as Bishop Philbin of Down and Connor has said, the false image of the Church as concerned uniquely with an after-life is widespread. But if this image is widespread, it is likely that there is some reason for it being so. Is it not possible that morality has been likened to cultivating one's own garden to the exclusion or at least ignoring of anyone else's? Christian charity has not been presented as a force which goads us on, as it was for Saint Paul: 'the love of Christ goads me on'.

There is nothing specifically irresponsible in

Christianity; but Christians, like other men, can be irresponsible. And once they abdicate their responsibility, they can invent reasons to justify themselves. They can falsify the notion of the providence of God to suit their own laziness and greed. They can substitute a false notion of the will of God to cover up their lack of hunger and thirst after justice.

Again, there always have been men and women, and there still are men and women in every walk of life who have accepted the responsibility entailed by their belief in Christ. These can be our models, for in them we see what can be achieved.

Christianity, faith in Christ, makes demands on us. Are these demands any greater or less than those made on non-believers? In other words, is the Christian any less a man than an atheist? Responsibility is fundamentally human; but what a man is, in the concrete, responsible for, depends on the concrete situation in which he finds himself. Now, belief in Christ brings with it a belief in another dimension of the concrete situation. The world is not only a world in which justice is sadly lacking, but also a world which has been redeemed by Jesus Christ. The concrete situation of every man coming into this world is not only that he must die, but that he must rise again. This new dimension, far from subtracting from responsibility, adds to it. The responsibility of the atheist is necessarily incomplete, because he is not aware of the whole reality. But this is not by any means to claim that the Christian's responsibility is necessarily complete; the claim is that he has a greater responsibility to live up to. That the atheist can live up to his responsibility better than the Christian lives up to his, is true; further this possibility may often be realized. The words of Saint Augustine, 'Many are within who seem without, and many outside who appear to be inside,' are echoed by Martin Buber: 'The atheist staring from his attic window is often nearer to God than the believer caught up in his own false image of God'.

Christian responsibility then is an extension of fundamental human responsibility. In this book is set out how modern atheistic thought has developed this basic notion of responsibility. I think that we can learn from this development.

GARRET BARDEN, S.J.

*Heythrop College*
*Oxfordshire*

# I

## *The Meaning of Modern Atheism*

Nietzsche spoke of the death of God, and the theme became a catch-phrase. But it was not Nietzsche's invention, nor should it come as such a shock to Christians. Faith, hope and charity are based on a fact; a fact which includes the death of God and his victory over death. God is risen! What surprised the ancient world—and we too easily forget this—was not that God was dead, but that, once and for all, he had risen from the dead. For the Stoics the death and rebirth of God was a never-ending process. At the close of each great cosmic year everything was renewed; the eternal return ruled the cycle of birth and death. Weighed down with this monotony, ancient people sought a God who would die but once, and thus accomplish the mystery of a true transcendence which would be impassible no longer because it had undergone real death.

Doubtless, when we think nowadays of the death of God, our meaning is very different. For we no longer mean a true death, but refer rather to the disappearance of the idea of God from among men. The theme of the death of God is not just another more modern name for the problem of atheism. But the juxtaposition of these two meanings is not without reason, for they are less alien to each other than a first glance would lead one to believe. The true atheist is the man for whom God is totally and finally dead. Nietzsche did not mean, as some erroneous interpretations would have it, that man should kill God. He meant rather that God was already dead, despite men's efforts to ignore the fact. He meant that men had killed God unwittingly, and that now, terrified by their act, they were seeking to forget it, refusing to take the responsibility for it and continuing their lives as if nothing had happened. Thus, because of an act for which they repudiated the responsibility, men had become prey to a morbid sense of guilt. Atheism, guilt, resentment—these three are related in Nietzsche's mind. We cannot afford to ignore this association, if we wish to understand one of the essential elements in the denial of God.

On the other hand, the theme of the death of God is no longer in the forefront of atheist thinking. To many it now seems as ridiculous to attempt to prove the non-existence as the existence of God. In the nineteenth century atheism passed from the intellectual to the existential plane; in Proudhon's terms it became anti-theism. But the struggle against God springs from and presupposes belief in God. Anti-apologetics presupposes apologetics; anti-theology, theology. For this very reason the most vital and the deepest currents in contemporary atheism tend to place themselves beyond the problem of God. And if we are to understand it, we must study it in this paradoxical situation. For some God is no problem. Replying to a survey carried out by *L'Age Nouveau* in January 1955, René Lalou wrote: 'For me the subject holds no attractions. God interests me only in so far as he is a human invention which has some great art and fine poetry'. The problem of God is thus reduced to the status of a human belief to be explained by psychology, history, or sociology. It is remarkable that the vast majority of the replies to this survey can be clearly divided into two classes. On the one hand, those who deny our need of God; on the other, those who affirm it. However, the latter invariably open with a denial of the validity of any proof of God's existence. Nonetheless, the most fundamental criticism goes beyond this stage only to eliminate the problem by showing it to be without interest or importance for the man of today. No matter what solution men happen to give to the problem of God, it is not over this that they are divided. Belief and unbelief no longer rule men's actions in any significant way. 'Why attack the idea of God?'

asks Maurice Nadeau.[1] 'It seems quite capable of falling apart of its own accord. It is dangerous only on the level of historical and social development. For development takes place under the influence of struggles far removed from those of reason and belief. It seems to me of very little moment that employer and employee, both Christians, meet in the same church. It is not in church, but in the factory, that their real life is found.' Atheism is then sometimes no more than the denial of a problem which, were it a real one, would be the most pressing of all. But the problem of God can be pronounced unreal and mythical, for it no longer divides men. As Yvon Belaval puts it: 'Can you imagine such a survey as this in the nineteenth century, or among Moslems? That it is possible, rather that it is taken for granted, among us, is the most cogent proof of the complete disappearance of belief, even from among believers'.

When we try to systematize these positions in order to discover their underlying structure, we come upon the following characteristics. Once God has been eliminated only man remains. What is important for man, is the way in which he faces the changing situations which confront him. The question of God is either mythical or theological; and philosophy, by the very fact that it must

[1] *L'Age Nouveau*, Paris 1955, 91.

become wholly human, is clarified by the ending of theology. Modern atheism is no longer the conclusion, but the starting-point of a search. It is the situation in which man finds himself, and, consequently, the situation in which he must think and act. Atheism is not a discovery, but a datum. When Marx wrote that atheism would be transcended, he meant that communism would be able to consider the non-existence of God as granted, and so be free to take the existence of man as its starting-point. 'Precisely because man has become visible and perceptible in nature,' wrote Marx in his *Political Economy and Philosophy*, 'it has become almost impossible to ask if there exists another being whose nature is above that of man. For that question implies the contingent character of both nature and man. Atheism, inasmuch as it denies this contingence, is meaningless, for atheism is the negation of God, and by that very negation it affirms the existence of man. But socialism as such has no longer any need of this reflection; it has its source in the knowledge, both theoretical and practical, of man in nature considered as Being.' We must take note of the fact that here we have a traditional position overthrown. It is true in general, at least among western peoples, that theism, regardless of its particular form, was, so to speak, the 'done thing'. Those who denied God, placed themselves beyond the pale of at least the greater part of society. In every sense their attitude was uncommon. Although based on a strong materialistic tradition, it was, nonetheless, narrow and limited. To turn atheist was to cut oneself off—often as much by behaviour as by thought. Atheism demanded reading and leisure, a hyper-intellectual attitude and a disdain of the common people. 'Atheism,' remarked Robespierre, 'is aristocratic'; and because he hated aristocrats, he hated atheists also. However, during the course of the nineteenth century from being aristocratic and intellectual, atheism became democratic and political.

For millions today atheism is a way of life. The atheistic world of today is not the brain-child of the materialist philosophers. It is, rather, the product of a historical situation. In an excellent article *Signification de l'Atheisme*[2] P. Jolif expresses the same idea very well: 'It (atheism) appears as the method by which humanity will endeavour to rid itself of some of the evils embedded in daily life: hunger, war, injustice. It is lived by the masses as a hope and an effort, before it becomes a system of the philosophers. It may even be true to say that first there are the questions confronting man concerning his very existence and that only afterwards is there the rejection of God, who is, we should say, indispensable if these same questions are to be

[2]*Economie et Humanisme*, Paris 1956 (May-June).

answered'. A study of atheism can no longer content itself with an examination of an abstract concept in order to show that it lacks both coherence and foundation. To study atheism is to turn to the present condition of man. Atheism is a system of living values. One cannot overcome it without understanding these values, without living them as far as is possible, without establishing, by living them, that to accept them does not imply the rejection of God. In this chapter we intend to analyse the actual situation of the atheistic world; we shall do so under three headings which, for convenience, can be labelled, Scientific Humanism, Political Humanism, and Ethical Humanism. Although we do not wish systematically to ignore philosophical considerations of the question, nonetheless they shall be introduced only to clarify concrete attitudes.

## I. SCIENTIFIC HUMANISM

It is by now generally accepted, at least by Christians, that the conflict between science and religion is dead and buried, and that it cannot rise again, because these two things occupy entirely different worlds without ever coming into contact with each other. The age of scientism is past. But perhaps that attitude is too optimistic, too naïve. It takes no account of the spirit of modern science, nor of the vital exigencies of faith. Rather than bask in a false security let us examine these questions more closely, and analyse more exactly the demands, the spirit and the suppositions of science.

Traditionally, science was a way to God. *Coeli enarrent Dei gloriam.* By an ever deepening understanding of the marvels of the universe man was able to offer them in homage to God, their Creator, while at the same time he deepened and purified his knowledge of him. This attitude was superseded. A more demanding one took its place, abandoned this facile view and demanded the separation of the two orders. Science is autonomous in its domain, so the theory ran; but its domain is not inclusive, and it must not mistake itself for morality or philosophy or religion. However, this juxtaposition is too easy. There is not on the one hand the phenomenal world, and on the other the noumenal, with no link between the two. In one sense the noumena are in the phenomena, and science, without crossing its boundaries, does attain the real. As P. Russo remarked in his short *History of Scientific Thought*, the reaction which occurred at the turn of the century against scientism—Poincaré's pragmatism, Duhem's efforts to show that science remained at the surface of things without reaching their essence—afforded but false security. For these ideas failed to exhaust the meaning and scope of science. Today science is surer of itself, and it is difficult to claim that it does not get at the heart of reality. Furthermore, scientific development has forced man to consider the problem of his nature, has forced him to ask himself what he might be. More than philosophy, more even than religion perhaps, it is science which confronts humanity with the question of its being and destiny. And science, because of its spirit and method, places this question within this universe; here and now science attains the real; here and now it wishes to assure man's destiny. Thus another spirit, a new mentality is forged. It will bear closer scrutiny.

The first of the traditional beliefs questioned by classical science was the passage from this world to God. Schematically we could say that if philosophy retained the God of reason, science rejected the God of explanation. As early as the Epicureans two things were demanded of a scientific hypothesis: it should take account of all the evidence; it should not pretend to explain obscurities by recourse to the intervention of the gods. This was, so to speak, the first methodological atheism. Renouvier likewise called atheism the true scientific method.

For the scientist engaged upon his research the real, by definition, is whatever can be examined, and the true is whatever can be affirmed in accordance with his methods. Reality is not what is observed, but what can be verified. In place of 'objects' science has 'phenomena'. Scientific laws express the relations between these phenomena rather than the intrinsic properties of the objects. But in the final analysis this knowledge culminates in a control over the objects of our experience. This control is the guarantee of our knowledge. The goal of science is to explain the diverse conditions of the world by their relations among themselves. Science does not consider the world as a whole, but rather takes the world as a datum and, following its principles, is limited to it. Scientific immanentism is radical. As Montesquieu put it, every scientific effort to evolve a systematic explanation of the world is immediately suspect of atheism. 'I do not know why,' he wrote, 'but it seems impossible to work out a systematic account of the world without being accused of atheism. Descartes, Newton, Malbranche, Gassendi, are but a few examples of those who tried. And this accusation serves only to strengthen the position of atheism, since it leads one to believe that atheism is so natural to man, that all systems, despite their great internal differences, tend towards it' (*Mes Pensées*). Science forbids her followers to treat the universe as an object whose maker is yet to be found. In Kantian terms, we have no right to make a transcendental application of the principle of causality. Because it is valid within the universe, it does not necessarily follow that it is valid of the universe. Lachelier wrote: 'I am guilty of a paralogism, if I pretend to have inferred the existence of God from a consideration of the universe in the manner of a physicist who infers the cause from the effect. Doubtless every effect demands a cause, but a cause of the same order as itself—at least this is as far as we can go from a consideration of the laws of our understanding.' Furthermore it is certainly true that by no longer using God as an explanation of uncertain cases we purify our notion of him. For to prove God scientifically is to reduce him to being the first link in an explanatory chain, thus making him homogeneous with the rest of the explanation, an object rather than a subject. Deism, as Voltaire understood it, is the worst denial of God. It is in this sense that Gabriel Marcel was right in claiming that the application of the principle of causality to God was the primary source of atheism.

Inversely, as P. Sertillanges has it, science, by excluding God from its domain, opened the way to a higher, more moral and more spiritual conception of him. 'Science has forced the abdication of the sun-god, the sky-god and the dragon of the eclipse, in short of all religious jujus. Science has eliminated shamans, witch-doctors and oracles. It has contributed to the purification of the idea of

God among Christians. For this much we should be grateful.' And this is no small advantage. But what science discovers, we do not call God. However the advantage is ambivalent. If, for some, the idea of God is purified, for many, to whom the old and revered argument from causality[3] was a great source of security, God has become more remote.

Besides, the advantage is a gift of long standing, and the faith of educated Christians has long ago assimilated it. But modern science presents other difficulties and creates a climate and mentality favourable to atheism. In his study of the 'Christian Consciousness and the Universe'[4] P. Dubarle effectively illustrates this fact. In the course of centuries science has undermined what he calls 'the causal way of thinking'. This is perhaps the most important element in the scientific revolution. Movement is no longer regarded as requiring an extra-material cause, a kind of spiritual motor. The energy responsible for movement is inherent in the universe itself, and is conserved and transmitted according to the inter-relations of things themselves in conformity with laws which permit the

[3]Needless to add, the word 'cause' is taken in its scientific and modern meaning. The question of the validity of the proof of the existence of God by a metaphysical consideration of the insufficiency of the world—a consideration which Spir has termed a 'systematic deception'—remains open.

[4]*Lumière et Vie*, September 1954.

calculation of the resulting phenomena. What took place during the seventeenth century with respect to energy and motion, is today being re-enacted with respect to the whole organization of forms and functions. Whatever way the universe is explained, at least no one denies that it is in process of development. Modern scientific theories are theories of expansion. Galaxies too have their formation and genesis. The success of the theory of the expanding universe is well known. Each of the several evolutionary theories stresses the genesis of our world, the groping development of life, the final emergence of man, himself in evolution. Furthermore, everything is explained in virtue of the initial datum. Whatever the details of the emergent scheme may turn out to be, there will be no need to introduce at any stage a supra-natural cause. Everything is so well explained in fact, that the scientist is embarrassed by the question whether it may be claimed that material nature is the sufficient principle of everything that exists, and whether the higher grades of being which have evolved may be no more than a particular perfection of a possibility inherent in matter itself. P. Dubarle formulates the question in cogent terms: 'Scientific thought in the present day is taking a step forward. The organization of the world no longer seems to demand a cause of energy and movement beyond the universe. Physicomechanical energy is allowed to play an "informing" role in the emergence of the world. The production of organized systems, the appearance of functions directed by what can be called finality, are to be firmly placed, with few restrictions, within the scope of the natural possibilities of the universe. There is no necessity for a reflection which would place some superior principle at the origin of things. One need only consider the natural possibilities and properties of matter. Informed scientific thought allows the world a new self-sufficiency.'

There is yet another aspect of science which tends to develop the atheistic way of life and thought. It would be unjust to call it a will to power. Nonetheless, because of its ever-increasing involvement with technique—both as a matter of fact and of principle—science tends to produce a state of mind which would at once explain and dominate the universe. It is an attitude which is in the fullest sense humanist, but which, nevertheless, seems ill at ease with other contemporary brands of humanism of different origin. The conditions of future application—the *praxis*, if you will—are embodied in the essence of theory. A concept is scientific inasmuch as it is technical, that is, insofar as it is capable of application. Modern science, having destroyed the contemplative mentality, has replaced it by an attitude of effective explanation.

By penetrating increasingly what Bacon called the secret arrangements of nature, by understanding them from within as well as by putting them to its own use, by adapting itself even to the point of casting doubt on the validity of its own principles in order to grasp more accurately an infinitely complex and subtle reality, the human spirit does not prove the non-existence of God, but it ceases to experience any need of him. The scientist does not contemplate the intelligibility of God; he creates the intelligibility of the world. This method of knowing, because of its honesty and rigour, tends to scorn all other methods, especially philosophical reflection and religious faith, which appear vague, subjective, even dishonest. Scientism is not dead. Those who claim that it is, have in mind the form which it took in the nineteenth century, and that certainly has gone, but only to give place to a new scientism. For what, after all, is scientism if not the conviction that all knowledge is homogeneous? And this conviction, which means in practice that there is only one authentic form of knowledge, is far from being a relic of the past. Modern man feels that, by the union of science and technique, he can unite himself with nature, collaborate in some way in her evolution and thus transform natural history into human history. He finds fault with those who refuse to take into their hands the destiny of the world and of man. From this viewpoint atheism is more than a methodology; it is a new humanism. The atheist is he who assumes the responsibility of the world and of humanity, and who takes the only efficacious means to accomplish his task. Atheism appears as the willingness to assume human responsibility to the full.

These considerations can lead us to a clearer realization of the extent to which the relationship between man and nature has changed throughout the ages. Three recent revolutions in industry—the first ushered in by the development of the internal combustion engine, the second dominated by the practical applications of electricity, the third, which is taking place in our own time, to be characterized, no doubt, by the harnessing of atomic energy—have all had the same effect. Each one has contributed to the change from the 'natural milieu' of pre-mechanistic society to the 'technological milieu' created by man himself. For thousands of years men lived in close contact with nature. Theirs was a civilization of peasant and artisan. Their lives were enclosed in the rhythm of humanity, in the rhythm of the world itself. The man of the natural milieu is in deep harmony with the elements and seasons. Nature, according to Friedmann, evokes in us such attitudes as closeness to the real, contact with the elements, sympathy with persons and things. In those days people thought in a rural, not an urban idiom. The galloping horse was the measure of speed. In direct contact with water, earth and beast the human body succeeded in imposing its own rhythm on life and work. Time moved in a stream, calm and limitless. In such a world 'know-how' was always accompanied by sympathy for all creatures. That such a world was a creature of God, was an easy and natural consequence. It was an object of love and respect. Man became meditative before it. The desert for Renan was monotheist. And it has often been said that the country inspires belief in God, but the city, belief in man.

Day by day the traditional countryside disappears. It is becoming urbanized, mechanized like a city. Man receives the natural world as a gift, but he feels and knows himself to be the creator of the technical world. In Christian tradition the universe is the sign of God, the work of his hands. In his article on the meaning of atheism P. Jolif recalls how for the Middle Ages the world was transparent, opening out to God. Plato had taught the Church Fathers the law of universal exemplarism: all things are the symbol, the sign of God. The Bible is a supernatural, the world, a natural revelation. 'The created world,' wrote Saint Bonaventure, 'is a book wherein we may read the creative Trinity. It is a resplendent mirror showing forth the wisdom of God.' Today the world is shorn of its sacred character. In it man finds, not God, but himself. Descartes recognized this when he retained the analogy between God and man, but rejected that between God and nature. The Cartesian proofs of the existence of God are based on his 'idea', whether considered in itself or in the human mind. The human spirit, unlike the universe, still retains, for Descartes, the mark of its Creator. In losing its sacred character the world took on a human form. We have already remarked on the asceticism and purification needed to effect this change. It has also been pointed out how it was Christianity itself which first gave the world to men: The world is for you; you are for Christ; Christ is for God. But in fact the Jewish religion had already done this. The universe of the Bible is already secular. The distinction between the uncreated divine order and the created order is clearly recognized. Thus the old pagans persecuted the Jews and Christians for their 'atheism'. Still, the Judeo-Christian world was created and bore the imprint of its Creator. Now that too is passing away. Space no longer inspires awe, but the spirit of conquest. Further removed from the world the idea of God has become purified for the reflective mind. For the common imagination he is merely infinitely far away. This may explain the acceptance of Teilhard de Chardin, for he was able to rebuild the temple of the universe. At all events, in as much as it substitutes activity for contemplation, insofar as it exploits human responsibility to the limit, scientific humanism rejoins the other currents of contemporary thought to which we must now turn.

## 2. POLITICAL HUMANISM

Jacques Maritain has remarked that during the last hundred years or so the storm of atheism has burst upon the history of humanity. This atheism is both absolute and positive; absolute, for it truly denies God himself; positive, for it is an authentic anti-theism. It is an atheism which demands total commitment, and which would change the face of the earth. It appears as a radical humanism, as a tremendous effort on man's part to possess his humanity completely. God is thought of as an obstacle to be brushed aside. To be more specific, during the past hundred and fifty years a world which has been wrongly labelled 'dechristianized' or 'pagan', has made its appearance. In fact, it has been born outside the Church and her semi-feudal, semi-bourgeois structure. The correct description of this world is simply 'atheist'. For in it there is an instinctive mistrust of all who affirm the existence of God, only, as is thought, the better to impose their authority on their fellows. 'He who speaks to me of God,' cried Proudhon, 'wants either my money or my life.' No doubt the political dimension is an essential one. But for centuries it was the exclusive affair of the few—a ruling individual, family, caste or class. Ours is the age of the birth of political consciousness among the many. Everyone is becoming increasingly aware of his political identity. God appears as an artifice which the rulers used in the past to keep the majority in an unending political adolescence, and thus to prevent their reaching full development. God is the stumbling-block which must be cleared from the road. That they may the better affirm their own existence and give it meaning and value, many today feel constrained to deny the existence of God. Of course, it may also be true that men, in perpetual contact with and, as it were, vowed to the production of material wealth, are naturally atheist. Their mentality is conditioned by their own transformation of nature, and by their own creation of goods useful to the progress of the human race. Their culture is built on what they create; it is political, economic, social. True enough, they might find God in other ways, in their thirst for justice, for instance. In fact, it is in their very thirst for justice that they are led to atheism in the first place. At all events, the problem of God, when it occurs, occurs in an economic and social context. Proudhon, in his *Contradictions Economiques*, considered it necessary to include a chapter on—or rather, against—God. Is this not symbolic of an important crisis in the development of humanity? The problem of God has become democratic. It no longer has its source in the aristocratic science of ideas, metaphysics, but in the democratic science of human needs, in the science of work, political economics. Henceforth, man's ultimate and strictly religious options are no more than a function of his material and social situation.

Further, this mentality is not the exclusive property of the working class; it is common to all classes. It is reinforced by the demiurgic aspect of modern science. Contemporary atheism is directly linked to the crisis and the critique of wisdom. Create, and by creating create yourself. Lequier's original maxim but soon taken up by Renouvier, is claimed today by existentialist and Marxist alike. For today a great part of humanity is more concerned to transform than to explain. Many are of the opinion that there can be no explanation without transformation, that the two are inextricably bound together. The notion of science as no longer 'vain and empty, merely contemplative'—Descartes' phrase—but as that which will give us 'the dominion and possession of nature', depreciates the God of explanation, and creates besides a mentality for which recourse to God in any circumstances whatsoever is less natural and spontaneous than before. In this respect the danger increases with the development of the so-called human sciences. For here, more than anywhere, the liaison between knowledge and action is particularly close and tenacious. It is these sciences especially which tend to convince man that he has grasped the fullness of his destiny. It is certainly true that in the United States certain forms of sociology and psycho-analysis combine to create a mentality which, if not atheist in principle, at least in practice rejects all true religious experience, and ends up as some brand of naturalism. These many diverse causes induce most people to see wisdom as the attitude of the impotent, who, incapable of action, turn in upon themselves and upon God. In a sense one becomes wise by becoming powerless. Then one makes a virtue of necessity, and powerlessness is considered virtuous. It is true that not all wisdom is Christian, or even theist. Often enough it has been contrasted with holiness. Nonetheless, the notion of wisdom seems to imply at one and the same time a certain detachment from the immediate, a capacity to stand back from the world and to make contact with some superior being, some God. Even pantheistic wisdom supposes a detachment of some sort from the *natura naturata*, some progress in the knowledge of and communion with the impersonal principle which can unite spirits in truth. In short, it presumes a higher degree of knowledge or contemplation. For Spinoza, as for the Stoics of old, there is the same distinction between the wise man and the fool. The wise man is he who knows, and acts well because he knows. His self-sufficiency, his *autarcheia*, is born of his knowledge. Contrariwise, for most people today the primacy of action is total and absolute. Here for instance is the rupture between Hegel and Marx. Heir of classical philosophy, Hegel thought that man could find satisfaction in wisdom, which he identified with the absolute idea or absolute knowledge. Man, at first alienated, is at last reconciled with nature when he has understood it. For Marx, on the other hand, man is satisfied only by the effective transformation of the world. There is no way besides that of *praxis*. Wisdom is not to be found beyond history, and the notion of a culture detached from or exterior to history coincides with the notion of a culture both effete and useless. Precisely because of this desire to be present to the event, it may not be incorrect to define certain aspects of contemporary atheism as the rejection of everything which smacks of what is considered bogus wisdom.

This attitude led Marx to an atheism which was not merely the superstructure of his doctrine, but an essential component of it. He defends his position with two arguments, which are, in fact, of unequal worth. The first and better known is sociological and somewhat exterior. Religion is the 'opium of the people', is the well-known slogan; but its context is often ignored. 'Religious misery is at once an expression of real misery and a protest against it. Religion is the cry of the down-trodden. It is the heart of a world without a heart, the spirit of an age without a soul. It is the opium of the people.' Because this world is not adequate to assure man of his complete accomplishment and integrated development, he compensates himself with the image of another, more perfect world. Religious alienation has its source in economic alienation; remove the latter and the former vanishes. Religion, according to Engels, is the act by which man empties himself of his true self, and transforms the essence of his humanity into the phantom of an unknown god in the great beyond. Accordingly, atheism becomes positive, for it affirms the concrete and present humanity of man. Through the denial of God man is given back to himself, and is enabled to master his real being. 'Religion is but the illusory sun which circles around man—unless he becomes his own sun.' In this sense, as we remarked at the outset, Marxism, instead of being atheistic, transcends atheism. Atheism is a presupposition; it is considered as a negative and already fulfilled condition which allows man to take himself as starting-point, himself as he concretely is. Humanity must look to its own destiny. It must neither worship the nature of which it is itself the summit, nor must it make man into a god, for man has issued from nature. Finally, it must not postulate a mythical supernatural in opposition to the natural. The communist is neither religious nor impious, for impiety is a function of religion. The basic error of even the best-intentioned spiritual ideas is revealed by their twofold incapacity to foresee and to direct political events. All social action is ineffective insofar as it is spiritual.

The essential of Marxism, however, is less the critique of theism and Christian spiritualism of every kind, including idealism, than the fundamental affirmation which identifies atheism and liberty, or rather, liberation. Marx based his atheism on his conception of work. Because man is his own demiurge, that is, because he makes himself human through his struggle with nature, it is impossible that he should have been made by another, a God. Marx's atheism is the inevitable corollary of positive definition of man as a working being who enters into his humanity by transforming the world. Freedom is to be of oneself; to be free is to be independent of all that is not self. Accordingly, either man is created by and dependent upon some other, and so not free, or else he holds his being from himself and so is free. But if man has his existence from himself, then God cannot exist. The problem thus appears as one concerned with the ultimate nature of freedom—of that freedom which the young Marx referred to as 'the eternal aristocracy of human nature'. Marx recognized these consequences: 'No being is independent in its own eyes, unless it is sufficient unto itself; and it is not sufficient unto itself, unless it holds its own existence from itself. A man who lives by the grace of another man, considers himself dependent. But I live completely by the grace of another when I owe to him, not only the conservation of my life, but also its very origin and source. The source of my life is of necessity outside myself if I am not my own creator. For this reason it is difficult to rid the popular imagination of the idea of creation. The socialist, on the other hand, since for him all history is no more than the creation of man by work, no more than the gradual overcoming of nature by man, possesses the visible and irrefutable proof of the fact that he is his own creator. For he sees the processes of his own creating'. From the first, Marx made his own the defiant cry of Prometheus: 'Philosophy does not reject, but makes its own the creed of Prometheus. In a word, I detest all the gods! This motto is to be set against all the gods of heaven and earth who do not recognize human consciousness as the supreme divinity'. Such was Marx's thought while he was still a liberal philosopher. On this subject the mature works will supply a double and complementary development. The more religious a man is, the less is he a man; the more a man is a man, the less religious will he be. It is interesting to note the connection between religion on the one hand, and economics and politics on the other. God is not questioned in himself; rather the nature of the relation between God and human existence is exposed and rejected. To quote Marx once more: 'the critique of heaven becomes a critique of the world; the critique of religion, the critique of law; and the critique of theology, the critique of politics'. We may add, in passing, that, despite their differences, both Marx and Nietzsche evolved the same method, the importance of which cannot be overestimated. System was no longer to be opposed to system, nor was a system to be criticized from the point of view of its internal coherence. No! a system was to be destroyed by being uprooted completely; its human—and all too human—roots were to be laid bare. Marx analysed the collective and social conditioning of knowledge, Nietzsche the individual and psychological. The question of sub-structure—or of sub-structures—became dominant, until today we cannot omit the examination of the sub-structure of belief in God.

Finally, if we are to grasp the ultimate meaning of the Marxist criticism, we must consider the fact that this form of political atheism implies a real transformation of the meaning of truth. The most original element in Marx's thought is, perhaps, the notion that human truth is neither natural nor metaphysical, but, in the strictest sense, political, that is, mediated by history. If Marxism denies a noetic heaven, this is not in order to admit a manifested truth. For Marx truth is dialectic, truth is historical, because the political, as he understood, is the noblest dimension of human existence. Just as humanity must suppress private property which separates the bourgeois from the proletariat, so too it must suppress God who separates man from man. In brief, all are agreed that man's task is to reach his fellowman. The believer is he who thinks that God is necessary if man is to attain this end. Atheism denies this mediation, and so confronts man directly with man. 'Atheism,' wrote Marx, 'is humanism mediatized by the suppression of religion, and communism is humanism mediatized by the suppression of private property.' Marxism appears as the destroyer of the last remaining idols. The basic error is to believe in a value existing in itself, objective and imposing itself on man from the outside, while in reality it is of man's creation, the result of his work. Within the capitalist system, as within religion, man becomes the slave of his own works, for within the one the fetishism of merchandise and gold, and within the other the fetishism of the gods, hold sway. Man is alienated from himself because he is alienated from his works. Marx would restore him to himself. Man would then be able to reach full satisfaction, attain happiness by attaining a direct relation with other men, without the mediation of an illusory God. In Marxism the atheist becomes the man of this world, master of nature, by becoming purely and totally man.

### 3. Ethical Humanism

The attitudes which we have examined so far have this much in common. They are less concerned with proving the non-existence of God than with giving man power over his own being. In so far as their purpose is to persuade men to accept responsibility for themselves, they are supremely moral. Perhaps it is possible to define contemporary atheism by a twofold opposition on the one hand to the idea of wisdom, as we have seen, and on the other to licentiousness. The traditional atheist, at least in France, was a rebel both intellectually and morally, a Don Juan, a libertine. But the atheists of today are no longer libertines in the accepted sense of the term, and their ethical behaviour is hardly to be distinguished from that of Christians—a fact which poses some delicate questions for the latter! And they are certainly no libertines in that licentiousness, eroticism, and revolt seem to many to be an over-individualistic form of protest, too much attached to what it denies to be capable of producing anything new[5]. Indeed one facet of con-

[5]Needless to say, such a well entrenched tradition has not wholly disappeared. The work of Roger Vaillant is an example; he is a man of the eighteenth century; his atheism is aristocratic, Marxist neither in origin nor in character. Yet his preface to Laclos' *Liaisons Dangereuses* reveals to what extent even he is a moralist.

temporary atheism is the effort to accept, and even demand, both moral and intellectual constraints. This facet of atheism appears as a sort of classicism with its eagerness to bring to perfection those human virtues which are passing away. What but atheism gives birth to charity?, asks Camus. If the individual is the reflection of God, what does it matter if he is deprived of the love of man on earth, for one day he will have the fullness of love? But if he is a blind creature wandering in the shadows of a cruel and limited world, he has need of his fellows and their perishable love. True enough, some consider Camus's terminology religious and Christian in tone, and this leads them to look on his atheism with suspicion. If it is easy to find in some forms of atheism a renewal of stoicism—although in an entirely different metaphysical context and as pessimistic as the old Stoicism was optimistic—why blame God? One must simply act out one's life in a situation which in some way implies atheism. Here one can discern a contemporary method of dealing with the perennial problem of evil. The world is absurd, but man is not absurd, and because he is not absurd he must give meaning to the world. Absurdity would be the negation of man; but the absurdity of the world is the negation of God. Man finds himself in a dramatic situation, thrown without knowing why into an unintelligible universe, prey to every hardship and problem. The worst betrayal would be to attempt to justify an unjustifiable situation. All that is possible is to make do, more or less well, between men and by human means. To invoke God would be to desert. Anyway, of what use is such an invocation? There is no question of justifying evil; what is important is to fight against it. What possible advantage has the believer in this fight? As Francis Jeanson says, I must put my trust in nothing but myself and my fellows in the face of human hardship; my ethic is my own existence endangering itself almost unremittingly. Certainly I feel that I am being aided in this work of the building of humanity. I experience grace at all times. But this grace is nothing else but the precious aid afforded me by the love and co-operation of men. Atheism thus appears as an affirmation of freedom and a demand for responsibility. Thrown into a situation which he did not choose, the individual must be judged according to the way he acquits himself in it, that is according to purely human criteria. 'I shall choose to be free,' writes Jeanson, 'I shall choose to exist not in relation to God, but in relation with my brothers who share my predicament, even though their predicament may be worse than my own. Lest I betray this duty of solidarity I shall cast aside all other duties, all other obligations, even every other justice and love save those which I shall attempt to establish with them during this earthly life. If morality is possible, then it will not be lost in the venture; and if God exists, I am certain that he will be satisfied with this.'

Here then is a tentative definition of atheism by atheists themselves. To be an atheist is to live fully in relation not to God but to others; or, if a more abstract formula is required, atheism is for many a denial of theology in favour of anthropology. If Christianity is judged to be of some value, it is because it is readily understood as the affirmation of Christ to the accompaniment of the rejection of God. With Hegel theology does not disappear, but it loses its autonomous character; it is in some manner integrated with philosophy which becomes a meditation on theology whose truth and meaning it reveals. With Merleau-Ponty even this idea is missing, or, at most, remains as a polemical attitude exposing a contradiction between the religion of the Father, which is a theology, and the religion of the Son, which, by an inescapable dialectic, turns out to be an anthropology. Every theology appears falsely optimistic and superficially providential. By always seeking to unravel the knot of human drama by the appeal to some imaginary predetermined order, which is definitively the finality desired by the Father, theology excuses man from total responsibility for his own destiny. Contrariwise, anthropology places man's destiny squarely in his own hands. Men do not feel themselves brothers save when faced with a task of their own invention which they can freely accomplish. On this point, as on many others, there seems to be a clear distinction between Merleau-Ponty and Sartre. The former's denial seems more serene because more intellectual. In one sense Merleau-Ponty was an intellectualist; he had the passion to understand. Sartre, on the other hand, is a voluntarist, a moralist with a passion for action. Whence his more violent and frenzied style. Yet in both the basic inspiration is identical—the same rejection of theology in favour of anthropology, of metaphysics in favour of phenomenology. It is understandable that Sartre's ethics should be entitled *Man*!

Consequently the idea of sin is totally excluded. For if sin, in the literal sense, is sin before God, it is obvious that the denial of God implies the denial of sin—or, more accurately, it is the denial of sin which led to the denial of God. It is not enough to show that the loss of the sense of sin indicates the loss of the sense of God. This is true, especially outside Europe; the common denominator of Russian and American civilization is the loss of the sense of sin. But this loss is linked with the intellectual rejection of sin which is at the root of much contemporary thought. Atheism—to borrow the title of one of Hesnard's works—is the affirmation of *morality without sin*. Thus the whole notion of guilt is called in question.[6] In order that man may be

[6] This question is studied in further detail in 'Sinless Morality', p 64.

responsible for his behaviour in a particular situation, it is essential that the situation should not have been of his own making; he must not be guilty of it. The acceptance of responsibility is accompanied by the refusal of guilt. Atheism—and in this it is related to certain aspects of democracy—is an assertion of innocence. In short, the will for responsibility goes hand in hand with the refusal of guilt. Humanity is innocent, not, of course, in all the concrete circumstances of life, but radically, in the human condition itself. Atheism is a protest against the so-called myth of original sin. Precisely because man is not originally guilty, he is now responsible; because he is not guilty of his being, he must become responsible for his existence. Still, this responsible attitude is concerned with actions rather than intentions, with the exterior not the interior. Maybe here one can discover the clearest demarcation line between theism and atheism. For both there is a false interiority, which may be named 'being confronted with oneself'; and both reject it with equal vehemence. But for the atheist there is no alternative interiority, while for the believer the only true interiority is being confronted with God. The Christian has a twofold responsibility, that before God and that before History; whereas the atheist is responsible only before History. For the man of faith this situation carries with it the danger of a false interiority, retired within itself and centred on self. Many have fallen into this error. But correctly understood, Christian interiority remains open, reaching beyond itself towards God and towards other men. It has its own worth, its own being and structure. The notion of sin thus retains a profound meaning, although it should be admitted that this meaning is often ignored. The atheistic protest against a certain notion of original sin is justified because the notion is mythic, and is sometimes used to reassure men that their socio-economic predicament is the inevitable consequence of their guilt, and that they need not accept responsibility for it. At all events, the sentiment of guilt is at the core of the problem of modern atheism; and a certain infantile notion of guilt is one of the surest sources of the denial of God.

These attitudes are systematized and deepened in many contemporary philosophies, for example, those of Merleau-Ponty, Sartre, and Polin. Since we have already referred to Merleau-Ponty, we may take him once more as an example. We are concerned with only one aspect of his system, namely, his atheism, which, although he dislikes the term, would be, in the terms of Maine de Biran, a Defence (Merleau-Ponty uses the term Eulogy) of Philosophy. In fact, if he denies God it is not so much in order to affirm man, as to understand him. The Christian absolute, God, and the communist absolute, History, seem to him to destroy the problem—and the problem is myself, other men and the world. Man is fundamentally relative, and to use him as a peg for an absolute on which man will subsequently depend, is to misunderstand, even to destroy, man. Any attitude which postulates man's contingence only to derive it from an absolute and necessary being—which is to escape from contingence—is, in Merleau-Ponty's eyes, theological and a denial of philosophy. If philosophy is to be safeguarded it must be kept problematic, its hope must not be placed in any destiny, but rather in that part of man which is precisely without destiny. Either the absolute is absolute, and thus beyond our grasp; or else it is within ourselves, and thus shares in our finitude and contingence. Or perhaps, and this is more frequent than either alternative, the absolute is no more than an alibi, a mere expression which explains nothing, but which appears to dispense one from further enquiry. Metaphysical and moral conscience dies when it comes into contact with the absolute. God is useless; he is a foundation which is unknowable for 'any explanation of this foundation is contradictory, not with the fertile contradictions of human consciousness, but with the barren contradiction of inconsistant concepts'. Only my existence as an embodied consciousness allows me to understand how there gradually arises for me and for others a world of truth and values. The world is before us; it is always given, but as merely given it is unfulfilled and ambiguous. So it gives itself over to our activity which moulds and achieves it. We make the world and it makes us. The world is the result of our own and others' perceptions. These perceptions confront one another and meaning results. The world must not be sought elsewhere, but within this meaning which is both relative and perfectible. Thus every perception is at the same time singular and in concord with other perceptions. The idea of God destroys philosophy, for such an idea is a universal which would abolish all perspectives while pretending to offer them all together. It is a parasitic notion which arises from immanence, and which must be overcome by immanence. Morality consists in the honest search for accord with oneself and others, while eschewing as the ideal of accord every unreal and useless maxim which can serve only to halt the search by supposing the problem solved. The universe is nothing else but the fabric of meanings incessantly woven by human experience. Faithful to the intuition of the young Marx, as against the aberrations of his maturity, Merleau-Ponty defines the attitude of the philosopher by *praxis*, that is by the 'meaning which appears spontaneously within the concurrence of the actions by which men organize their relations with nature and with others'. The hypothesis, God, must be abandoned because it is no help, but rather a hindrance in understanding the inner meaning of human events. And if in a sense this attitude is more traditional, more philosophical and intellectual than some of the others we have studied, still it is in many respects analogous to them. For at the core of each is the refusal to believe that there exists somewhere an already perfected and ready-made system of things and ideas, the refusal to conceive an all-knowing and all-powerful Spirit for whom all problems are resolved and all dramas played out. At the core of each is the positive decision to assume day after day one's human task with no external guarantee, to create little by little truths and values in the struggle with nature and in one's relations with one's fellows, to transform knowledge itself by transposing the rationality of the concept to the heart of *praxis*, and finally to claim for humanity total responsibility for a destiny which is not written in advance, but which man himself must freely forge.

Close to this attitude, despite rather evident differences, is the attitude of Jules Vuillemin, one of the most vigorous of modern thinkers, who stands at the junction between existentialism and Marxism, while leaning more to the latter which he sees as a naturalism which is the goal of philosophic progress. For him too the choice is between 'philosophizing theology and philosophy—that is, atheistic humanism'. In his thesis *Être et le Travail*, he makes work the adequate link between man and being; he considers that the concrete analysis of the forms of work throughout history can alone furnish the solution to the ontological problem. Finally he opposes the perception of being through work to the emptiness of reflexive enterprises which never reveal more than the 'quasi-object of pure subjectivity'. Thus work is the guarantee that thought is objective. It resolves the problem of truth, 'because it becomes possible to turn to an energy that is both nature and foundation, consciousness of the object and consciousness of oneself, naturalization of man and humanization of nature—the power of work'. Since Lamark we know that to think is to respond to the demands of the environment. But the environment is not just given ready-made. Not only is it in continual evolution, but also, thanks to man's work, it is transformed and humanized; it ceases to be mere environment and becomes world; man is the being through whom evolution becomes history. There is no eternal environment. 'By history, nature is made the world of laws, a geographical and technical structure.' Work gives meaning to nature; it is the basic ontological act. We may go so far as to say that nature by man's economic activity, enters into meaning. History is time penetrating evolution from within; atheism is no more than the becoming aware of history. No longer is the subject on one side and the object on the other, both seeking a common base in God. By making it his partner, by forcing it to follow the vicissitudes of his own history, by acknowledging its temporal character, man confers on nature a new dignity. The ultimate basis is the existence of the historical man who has no need of eternity because he has understood time. This is the freedom of the man who wills and accomplishes the meaning of nature. The discovery of history is the death of God. 'That nature was constitutive and not merely materiality, that it was in the deepest sense reason and not merely law or rule, only atheism could discover when all the eternal commands and the voices of conscience had been silenced or at least put in question . . . Manifesting in us the new significance of nature, atheism likewise reveals the meaning of philosophy and the motivation of humanism' (*Deucalion*, IV; p. 45).

Finally, so as not to be too incomplete, just as there is a Christian mystique opposed to all moralism, so there is an atheistic mystique opposed to all morality. One atheistic tradition is based on the darker side of human personality, which opposes transdescendence to transcendence. This tradition, of Nietzschean origin and aristocratic in character, is at once close to and far removed from the themes we have been examining. It is close because it too wants to give back to man what he had lost in God.

Its motto is Nietzsche's phrase (it might well have come from Feurbach): 'Perhaps man will be able to raise himself up from the moment he is no longer engulfed in God' (*Gai Savoir*). But in its individual, psychological and almost asocial character this tradition is far removed from the others which we have studied so far. Christianity has always been blamed for subjecting man to God. Is there any reason why man should not be God? Or at least is there any reason why man should not descend into his own depths with never a thought or fear of reaching a limit? This is the meaning of Georges Battaille's *Expérience Intérieure*. Mysticism and sanctity are the greatest human experiences. But the Christian mystics have not savoured their experience to the full; on the contrary, they have limited it by doctrine, dogma and an ideological structure. If one would complete the journey to the limits of the possible, the mysticism of above and of being must yield to the mysticism of below, of non-being. One must seek out a kind of Godless holiness. The whole man in whom eroticism plays a vital part, without any mutilation, gives himself over to the nakedness of his own experience, without belief, without desire, without expectation. The night of mysticism is transformed into a radical non-knowing, which is nothing else but sheer experience, pure experience opening out into the unknown. All notion of revelation is rejected in favour of total clarity and sincerity. The discovery of oneself at the deepest possible level is its own end—even when the result is emptiness, nakedness, and utter solitude. 'I see the total nakedness of man, the depth of his stupidity, the condition of his sufficiency.' Disgust here would be a species of moral judgement, a stranger to pure experience. One must strip oneself of judgement as of hope in order to enter fully into experience. If one feels anguish in the emptiness of being, at least it will be the anguish of the superman who depends on nothing but himself. 'I will climb to the pinnacle... I insist that a sentiment of indefensible vanity is at the root of all this (just as humility is at the root of all Christian experience).' In a slightly different sense it could be shown that a pure and immediate perception of the sensible, a sort of communion with the non-rational, forms within the atheism of today a real reaction against the over-political and over-social forms of atheism, and could, tomorrow, develop into a true atheistic mysticism. At all events, contemporary atheism of this kind can be recognized by the fact that it has given back the original meaning to the term 'transcendence', which is no longer the term of some movement but the movement itself, the very act of going beyond. Thus contemporary atheism tends to define itself by a sort of immanent creativity, because it hopes to realize the cryptic promise of

Nietzsche: to emerge from emergence and in emergence, to go beyond oneself to the core of immanence.

## 4. Conclusion

Our intention has been not to question modern atheism in itself, still less to bring arguments against it, but to describe it at least partially, and to discover some of its fundamental tendencies. Nonetheless, by way of conclusion, it may be useful to add some remarks to guide anyone who wishes to distinguish between what is valid and what must be rejected. As a matter of fact millions today live by atheistic values; the believer cannot meet those people honestly unless he has some knowledge of these values.

Nowadays, as always, atheism serves as a purgative. In knowing one must distinguish between the representation and the intention. In a relative and finite being the representation of the absolute is necessarily relative, and the representation of the infinite is inevitably finite. All knowledge of God is permeated by inadequate representations. In all belief there is an unavoidable anthropomorphism. If God created man in his image, man has paid him back with interest, as Voltaire put it. This is neither surprising nor scandalous. Man can know nothing without some representation of the thing known, and this representation inevitably is limited to man's capacity. But the image should not be confounded with the thing. The image is no more than a means by which one can attain or conceive the thing. The essential is not the image, but that which the mind intends beyond the image. In all knowing negative judgement plays an important part. It forces knowing beyond itself; it opens it to a continual progress towards ever greater adequacy. Atheism plays the part of negative judgement in the knowledge of God. This enables us to understand how a philosopher like Lagneau, who abandoned all reflective analysis of God, was nonetheless able to assert that God did not exist. Perhaps during a period when God is excessively flaunted before men, at the cinema, in the theatre or in novels, it is good to recall believers to a certain modesty in this respect. Beyond all else we must refrain from attributing to God our own modes of feeling, thinking, existing. 'Atheist?', writes Giradoux in *Combat avec l'Ange*, 'Far from it! Existence is a terrible disappointment . . . To apply this notion of existence to God is as impious and false as to imagine God in our own image'. It is interesting to compare this with a phrase of Simone Weil's from *La Pesanteur et la Grâce:* 'I am certain that there is no God, in the sense that I am convinced that there is no reality which resembles anything that I can conceive when I pronounce the name, God'. And on the following page she has the suggestion: 'Of two human beings, neither of whom has had experience of God, the one who denies his existence is perhaps the closer to him'. Before attacking atheism every believer should seek to turn it to his own ends. It is difficult to attach too great an importance to that negative dialectic which attacks the all too human elements in our notion of God. More generally we must rediscover the tradition of negative theology, and learn at least this much from Kierkegaard, that there is a struggle between doubt and certitude at the heart of belief, because the dialectic between belief and unbelief cannot take place at any other level. It is rooted within, at the kernel of faith; it is an inner need of faith; it enables faith to become more aware of itself in the teeth of outside criticism. In recent times a too facile apologetic has tried to insist on the implicit belief of the unbeliever and to make him admit the existence of God in spite of himself. Perhaps the time has come to change the emphasis, and to stress rather the unbelief of the believer.

It does not follow that atheist criticism is always justified. Misunderstanding is the fault of both sides, and must be eliminated if the true differences are to appear clearly. Now, notwithstanding some unhappy expressions, it has rarely if ever occurred that Christianity, or indeed any truly philosophical theism (to be distinguished from Voltarian and other deisms) has conceived transcendence in a spatial manner, or has seen God as merely the maker or architect of the world. God is not the object of thought and experience, but that by which all thought and experience are possible. And one cannot escape from the consideration of that which all thought and experience imply.

The whole evolution of human knowledge reveals both the freedom and universality of the human spirit. Each new truth is, in one sense, a radical invention which could not have been foreseen and which is linked with its antecedents only later. Yet—and this is the truth of rationalism—a new truth is comprehensive, as Lichnerovicz saw; that is to say, that it cannot be deduced from its predecessors but includes them. The old does not become false, but incomplete. By its discoveries the human spirit does not contradict itself, but progresses and grows. There is a constancy and coherence of truth throughout history, not because the present is deduced from the past, but because it includes it. All this leads us to the distinction between the criterion and the guarantee of truth. The criterion is purely human. The confrontation of men throughout history constructs little by little the edifice of relative truths. It is possible that Descartes at the period of his *Regulae* thought that this edifice was self-sufficient. But he did not rest long in this belief. If he always thought that the purpose of human life, insofar as it was specifically human, was purely practical in the two meanings of that term, namely, mastery of self and mastery of the universe or morality and science, he also considered that this purpose was to be founded on reason, and that for this the *Meditations* were essential. The purpose of these was to assure the truth of human science and human wisdom. Science does not succeed in being its own foundation, in radically eliminating scepticism. So the *Meditations* are divided into two equal parts. With the hypothesis of universal doubt, how can man attain the truth? With the hypothesis of a God who is truth, how explain error? One could almost say, on the hypothesis of emptiness how explain plenitude? On the hypothesis of plenitude how explain emptiness (for plenitude is truth and emptiness error)? Once God has been recognized, man can pursue his task. The divine guarantee is not the criterion of truth; man must continue to fend for himself in the domain of natural knowledge; but he knows now that his knowledge is more than a well-constructed dream; he has put it on the level of reason. Thus, leaving aside any elementary Cartesianism, we can say that God may be conceived as the inspiration and the guarantor of that spirit of truth which moves humanity, and in which humanity moves. In the affirmation of the most relative truth there is the pretension of a universality, which is not the synthesis of all perspectives but the foundation of every perspective. At least the question is unescapable, and we have the right to expect atheists to examine it seriously.

We may recast our argument in different terms. To admit God is to refuse the absurd. We are not talking about absurdism. Neither Merleau-Ponty, nor Sartre, nor even Camus, professes an absurdism. If the world has no meaning, the same is not true of man. Man has meaning, and he cannot act without creating meaning. To declare that the world has no meaning, that our predicament is unintelligible, and that rooted as we are within it, we can nevertheless and ought to act well, is to take a courageous attitude, but it is not to escape the absurd. It is not enough to contend with meaning; meaning must be explained. It is true to say that much of modern philosophy, insofar as it is a refusal of God, is likewise a refusal of metaphysical explanation, and so a limitation of human experience. In our view, not the idea of God precisely, but belief in God is implied in the deepest and most elementary aspects of human behaviour, namely, confidence and humility. Confidence, which involves a certain vitality and interior control of self, is needed for both life and virtue. Humility is necessary, because the humility which expresses our ontological condition is, according to St Benedict, the truth of our relation with God, a truth which is recognized by intelligence and executed by will. In the same act, according to St Thomas, we must love ourselves, others and God. If philosophy is the description of integral experience, it should reveal the fact that the most elementary love of oneself implies love of God. Every act, like every thought, postulates an implicit faith in God. To think and to act is to think and to act in God. The choice is between faith and scepticism. The latter is, by definition, the refusal of faith of any kind. It is the sole true atheism. The sceptic refuses all meaning. Yet, though possible as a kind of game, scepticism is not possible as a way of life. Man's belief in God is in proportion to his rejection of scepticism. Everyone encounters the spirit of evil, and can overcome it only by faith in God. The world, according to African Spir, is a 'systematic deception'; and what is called a proof of God's existence, is based on the insufficiency of the world. Objective being does not exhaust being. We are in full agreement with Merleau-Ponty when he claims that the problem of the world is not solved by having recourse to God. The world as world answers for itself. But it does not answer for being. On the experiential level empirical being does not satisfy our demand for being. This is not fideism, but rather a vital and reflective attitude, a sort of implicit confidence which reflection must always explicitate. God who is thought last, is lived first. The absolute is revealed to us in two experiences: that of logical necessity which implies a link between our minds and God in the affirmation of every truth; and that of moral exigence which implies a link with God in every act of charity. To accept God is not to accept something given, but a giver. It is not to imagine that all problems are thereby solved, but to work towards a solution. It is not to believe that truth and goodness are ready-made, but to undertake to make them. The One, wrote Plotinus, is not so much the object of intelligence, as that by which the intelligence has objects. This implies that for the man of pure experience there is nothing but brute fact, while at the same time his acts confirm an implicit but unacknowledged belief in reason.

In general then contemporary atheism would be the full acceptance of the human condition. Man is a finite, contingent being who must work out his life in a situation which he has not created, who is yet responsible for himself and for others, who is unable to read his destiny in a book of wisdom in some noetic heaven, but is forced rather to work out his destiny in sorrow on this earth among men. To live according to atheistic values is to recognize this situation without trying to find an explanatory cause or an excuse for superiority, the emptiness of which is all too evident. The great merit of contemporary atheism is that it has achieved a scouring out of the human intellect by abolishing all idolatry. It does not turn man into a God, but fully accepts his humanity, and will answer for it. Never before has the human predicament been seen so clearly. For this atheism is not an abstract construction but a reflection arising from the concrete situation. Finitude, contingence, relativity, liberty, these are the common factors beneath the changing surface of man's life. Never before has the absolute been so utterly excluded. Nor should this displease the believer, for he should know better than anyone his own relativity, since he knows who is its foundation. God is not a ready-made answer, but the demand for an answer, and at the same time the guarantee that it is not absurd to seek one.

I am grateful to my atheist friends, for they have taught me not to cheat. Man is not God; this is not the whole truth, but it is the first and most indispensable. A radical critique of all human absolutes was needed, if the one true absolute was to be revealed. Too many believers have played at being God. It is good to purify our images so as to direct our aim more truly.

## 2

# *Sinless Morality*

In his *Morale sans Péché* Dr Hesnard implicitly raises the question of the relation between atheism and guilt. In this work he takes up and completes the central theme of his earlier book *L'Univers Morbide de la Faute*, namely, that man is above all an ethical being for whom moral exigence is fundamental. Man's basic need is for value; he is originally and radically an *être en valeur*, a being within a context of values. To claim that man is always *en situation* is to claim that he is constantly calling his own value into question at least by his actions even if not with his intellect. Every human drama, be it the most tragic exception or the everyday banality, is essentially a moral conflict, for in every instance the stake is one's own value. Man, as Hesnard understands him, does not live under the rubric of anxiety, or of sensuality or of power, but under the rubric of guilt: 'In everyone there is a bias toward guilt and self-accusation, which are the two primary human reactions connected with anxiety'. In this way the interpretation of the human psyche is given a new slant. Freud grasped it vaguely, but was prevented by the mechanistic framework of his thought from reaching and exploiting it. The fact that all human activity is immanently moral implies that psychosis or neurosis is expressive of a perversion or deviation of morality. The sickness of the mind is strictly a morbid sickness. There is no human activity which does not imply value. The neurotic has his own norms, even if these norms are aberrations. *Morale sans Péché* is the study of the relation between mental disease and morality.

There are methodological consequences of this; or rather, interpretation and method are closely allied. Method might be called 'doctrine in the making'. Hesnard has the merit of being at the junction of two streams, neither of which he is willing to abandon. Yet he is not content with mere juxtaposition; on the one hand, rationality and objectivity; on the other, the subjective and comprehensive element. Under pretext of rationality, a purely objective analysis is incapable of uncovering the human value of the clinical facts. Still, a phenomenological description of the illness from the patient's viewpoint is inadequate. What is called for is an 'objective understanding of the structure of conduct', to borrow a phrase from Ricœur. In other words the patient's attitude must be analysed as a whole embodying a meaning and significance which he himself has overlooked. So one comes to regard mental illness as an existence with some reference to culpability. Anxiety where there is no genuine danger, is fear of fault or punishment. Nervous collapse is both an effort and a failure to rid oneself of guilt; hysteria is an attempt to elude guilt through failure of bodily control; psychosis is the construction of an imaginary universe in which the patient tries to inculpate himself and others, or endeavours to live by foregoing his responsibilities, and so on. In brief, the refusal of genuine confrontation with one's environment leads to a sensation of guilt which one tries to shake off by whatever means are to hand. According to Hesnard, this is the morbid universe of sin. But who is to understand and interpret psychoses? Only the psychiatrist who, 'convinced of the fact that moral value is fundamental, sees in mental illness not the disorder of this or that function, but sees a human person who, since the emergence of his symptoms, lives within a universe of guilt'. For Marx the primary relation was between man and nature; for Hesnard, as it was for Hegel, the primary relation is between man and man. But more fundamental than the master-slave relation he discovers the relation judge-accused. 'The proof of your sin is your punishment,' cries the chaplain in Gide's adaptation of Kafka's *The Trial*. 'You must recognize your error, and become convinced of the fact: if I am punished, therefore I am guilty.' More paradoxically we can say: 'I punish myself, therefore I am guilty'. It is this Kafkaesque world of confused and diffuse guilt which constitutes for Hesnard the morbid universe of sin. In this novel the Jew who is arrested without knowing why or by whom, and who when released finally condemns himself, is the image of modern man. We live in the age of judge and defendant, executioner and victim—and these pairs unceasingly confront one another. In psychopathic and especially hallucinatory behaviour the patient lives out a drama of manifold and unexpected meanderings, but always with the same ethical theme. He tends less to accomplish his frustrated desires than to seek refuge in a world from which responsibility is excluded, where the anxiety of guilt will be lessened, and where his personal value of moral integrity can be restored. The sentiment of frustration, which in the last analysis is the sentiment of guilt, is transformed into aggression against both oneself and others. To condemn oneself is to refuse to accept oneself; and the refusal to accept oneself is the true name for mental disorder.

Dr Hesnard's psychology differs from Freud's in that it assumes a conflict of values rather than one of blind forces and impulses. The Freudian explanation is built around a mechanistic theory of instinctive and mutually opposed compulsions such as the life instinct or Eros, and the death instinct or aggression which are basic irreducibles. And when Freud shows that conflict is affective, he thinks of affectivity as quantitative and subject to purely physical laws. Whereas for Dr Hesnard the universe is immediately set within a context of values. The interpretation of illness as accusation, punishment, defence reaction is fundamental and primary. Dr Hesnard's hypothesis is then radically distinct from the Freudian theory; and those who hold the latter will be inclined to reject Dr Hesnard out of hand. Still, for present purposes it is not necessary to go into the relative validity of the opposing theories. Our immediate task is the elucidation of Dr Hesnard's theory which, notwithstanding the changes and modifications to be eventually introduced, is at least partially true. Although valid it is not exclusive; for in this more than in many other fields unilateralism must be avoided. Like tangled skeins, neuroses and psychoses can be unravelled by pulling on one of several loose ends. Dr Hesnard explains from above what Freud explains from below; and perhaps in the last analysis it is of little importance which is the more valid. One discovers a conflict of values where the other finds no more than the struggle of conflicting impulses. There is not necessarily any antinomy. And because the whole skein unwinds by pulling on the thread of morality, we must now examine the results of our efforts, not so much to discover the ethic of the abnormal, but to find what light it throws on the ethic of the normal.

Hesnard himself remarks that having undertaken some study of the abnormal he later applied what he had learnt to the normal, for it was the study of the abnormal which first allowed him 'to penetrate fully the internal structure of the concrete moral being'. It is in this sense that *Morale sans Péché* is the natural sequel to *L'Univers Morbide de la Faute*. The thesis of the later work is that ordinary morality, which he refers to as the morality or the mytho-morality of sin, has the same source and basically analogous characteristics. In their different manners the healthy man and the neurotic live in the same morbid universe. We put evil where there is none 'in a personal interiority, in the interior of the thinking being, who is thinking no longer as a prelude to action, but in order to contemplate himself in the grip of an often illusory guilt'. Rather than look for the fault in the action, we seek it in the interior of the person. This flight towards an inwardness which is sometimes painful and sometimes luxuriant, if not both together, shows up the irrealism of our ethic. The distinction, if not the opposition, between theoretic and lived morality is enough to reveal its mythic character. The high-sounding fictions of moral theory are no more than the camouflage for human aggression. Thus the common root of both normal and abnormal ethics is an illusory bad conscience, against which man must continually defend himself. This illusory conscience has its origin in what Dr Hesnard calls sin. By sin he means the private, interior, inward evil of the individual, the purely internal guilt, the fault divorced from the action. The more an individual is cut off from others, the more he feels himself a sinner, the greater is his sense of guilt. Often it is sufficient to do the deed, to perform the evil act, in order to rid oneself of the remorse for this kind of actionless sin. So much is this so indeed that 'sin persecutes above all those who have done nothing, who have sinned in thought alone, while it spares those who have accomplished the deed'. The radical mistake is to imagine that the origin of sin is not in doing but in being, for in this way one is liable to lay the blame on one's own or another's nature. The interiority of sin contains aggression in embryo, but it is an aggression separated from action. The more one rails against the nature of things, the less one comes to grips with real evils, the less one truly confronts men. One becomes the victim of psychological poisoning. Although Dr Hesnard is certainly opposed to the Nietzschean mentality, it is clear that his analysis goes along with that of Nietzsche on aggression and resentment. For him the common morality, whether in the normal or the abnormal individual, is the morality of sin and is, properly, an illusion.

In his attempt to explain this state of affairs Dr Hesnard outlines a cultural history of sin which, although interesting, is at least questionable, and is the weakest part of the work. In one chapter, 'The monotheistic myth of sin: a survival of animism', he throws the responsibility for the mytho-morality of sin on to Jewish and Christian monotheism, which have locked guilt within the heart of man by setting up a Tyrant who was to be supreme justice before whom men's desire must stand trial. Christ preached the true morality, 'an inter-personal ethic of love'. But his 'gentleness' has been almost wholly obscured by the vestiges of the jealous and avenging God of Israel, and later by the monastic ideal of contempt for life and instinct, and its desire for inward purity. The very idea of original sin implies some notion of a blemish in nature, a kind of evil inherent in the very existence of every man coming into this world. Original sin tends to develop a sense of guilt without responsibility. Men may begin to think that evil consists in their condition as men, and not in their mode of living and acting in concrete circumstances. In this manner the taboos of an animistic world have been enthroned in the individual himself. In any case, and whatever its origin, sin in Dr Hesnard's sense is composed of two elements: the interdictions of one's personal world and the myths of common thought. Sin is primitive taboo within the individual, where by 'primitive' is signified the childhood of both the person and the race. For Hesnard the fundamental discovery of psycho-analysis is not the grasp of the role of sexuality, but the understanding of the part played by childhood in the destiny of the individual. The child is truly the father of the man. In one sense the first exigence of morality is to free oneself from the Super-ego. As Dr Odier in his *Les Deux Sources, Consciente et Inconsciente, de la Vie Morale* remarks, the Super-ego is not strictly speaking moral but pseudo-moral. It is not an authority but rather a force which indifferently forbids or favours now evil, now good; now better, now worse. In terms which are not precisely his own, we could say that for Dr Hesnard there is on one side the individual and crowd-seeking aspect of man, while on the other is the realm of the person and true communication with another. To free oneself from sin is to escape from the infantile aspects of the individual, and from the mob instinct of closed society, and to reach the stage when the person in his every action coincides and harmonizes with the whole of humanity.

We can set out the essential elements of inner guilt under three heads: negativity; aggression; interiority.

1. We may begin with negativity. The mytho-morality of sin makes no positive demands but is

content with forbidding certain actions. According to Hesnard the chief characteristic of those whom he calls 'adepts of sin', lies not in what they do, but in what they leave undone, in other words, their never-ending flight from everyday responsibility. They are punished with a sadness which chases away all spontaneity. The denial of the joy of living leads to a hatred both of themselves and others. 'The interior anguish of guilt is more the result than the cause of the abandonment of the joy of living.' Guilt is felt as a stain, of which one can be rid only by expiation. The source of this negative attitude is an attitude of defiance against the real order, an attitude which condemns life and its instinctive joys. So much for negativity.

2. There is, in the second place, aggression. Interior sin is not merely a turning in upon self, a pure narcissism, but it is an active disapprobation of self, an aggression directed against oneself. The stages of the process can be grasped easily enough. Interior guilt is a refusal of self and consequently of life. This refusal of living is experienced as frustration which in its turn becomes self-accusation and aggression against self. Finally this denial of self ends in annihilation and death, unless it can be projected as aggression against others, and in this way become bearable. Aggression must not be set up as the indestructible opponent of concrete morality; we should look on it as the consequence

of the refusal of consent. It is not the deep-rooted instinct which Freud named the death-wish opposed to the will to live. Rather is it a perversion of the basic desire of men to communicate with others.[1]

3. Finally, there is interiority. This is the essential component which binds the others together. 'Sin' bends the individual back on his own being, cuts him off from action, and from sharing in the life and society of men. This interiority or inwardness can be called a lie, if a lie, at its deepest level, is the refusal of true relationship with others. Further, 'the sin of thought'—and confessors will admit this—often depends more on mental hygiene than on morality in the strict sense. Its world is a wholly subjective and egocentric world in which a man must finally suffocate. This suffocation is

[1]In his most recent work, *Psychanalyse du lien interhumain* (Paris 1957) Dr Hesnard takes up this idea of Politzer according to which the data of psycho-analysis are the set of facts which we call drama. For it is on the dramatic level that we communicate with others. It does not follow that we must admit the 'magnificent but mythic ambivalence' between the life and the death instinct in the Freudian sense any more than we are forced to admit a radically evil inclination at the base of human nature. Hesnard does recognize a fundamental concrete opposition, between Identification (or Participation or Communion) and Aggression. But Aggression which stems from a sociological or political mytho-ethic has none of the characteristics of 'sin'; it is derived from social conditions. Only Identification is primitive and natural. It exists in every man, and is a basic tendency to co-existence. Aggression is not a fatality but a breakdown; and the whole effort of civilization and culture is to restore in its perfection the primary and spontaneous inclination which we have named Identification.

itself morbid. The 'anxiety' of the 'sinner' is the harbinger and preparation for the 'anxiety' of the mentally unbalanced.

Against this mytho-morality of sin Hesnard favours authentic, or, as he prefers to call it, concrete morality. This ethic is not something new. And the author has no intention of founding it on his psycho-analysis. Psycho-analysis on the other hand can help to reveal it to us by showing up the inauthentic and morbid elements in contemporary morality. It shows that the kind of supernatural curse which weighs ever more heavily on the human condition, is no more than a myth from which we can free ourselves insofar as the progress of science shows its all too human mechanism. Just as Marx in the opening pages of *Das Kapital* analyses the uncanny objectivity of the laws of the capitalist system which weighs so heavily on the worker, but shows at the same time that these laws are of our own making and that their very existence is due to our idolatry, or, in his own terms, our fetishism which is the result of the reification of the laws; so Hesnard shows that 'sin' is certainly an objective reality, a reification if you will, but that this reification is our own doing, the result of our fetishism. But we can escape from its grip by understanding its immanent mechanism. If the sinner is he who lives in a state of anxiety, not on account of anything he has done, but on account of what he is or believes himself to be, then morality must be shorn of its mythic elements by a devaluation of thought and a revaluation of action as the norm of ethics. Basically ethics is simple. There is no need to look for its norms among heroes or saints; they are to be found in the commonest of experiences. Tolerate every idea, but proscribe every act which might damage another's person or, to put the same thing more positively, work for the 'ever-increasing perfection of human relations'. Concrete morality is that which unites a man with himself and with others. Inter-subjectivity is necessary for man; from the time he begins to think, perhaps even from the time when he begins to be, he identifies himself with his neighbour. This attitude reveals that his destiny is to be united with others. Instinctive drives, far from being condemned, are to be placed within a moral context. Our tradition and education combine to turn us in on ourselves and to lead to self-accusation—'It is my fault'—and later to accusation of others—'It is your fault'. 'Sin' is fear, a source of aggression, and hatred of self, others and life itself. Against certain forms of religious sentiment Hesnard makes the old charge of Epicurus and Lucretius that religion is the torment of men, the source of anxiety and fear. The religious soul, according to Lucretius, 'overcome with terror, applies the goad to itself, inflicts upon itself the sting of the lash, unable to see an end to its misfortunes, a limit to its chastisement, fearing rather that death will but aggravate the pain. For these fools, life on earth is as hell'.[2]

'Foolishness', or as Hesnard puts it, 'infantilism and archaism', along with terror and anguish, are the natural products of an education centred on guilt, which is to say, an education centred on 'myth', 'superstition', and 'sin'. Psycho-analysis would rid us of these scourges, and make us capable of creating the present and accomplishing the commandment of love. The most fundamental revolution is educational, and contemporary science allows us to develop from childhood to maturity. Epicurus as represented by Lucretius is a veritable god (*Ille deus fuit*), at the same time possessed of the true wisdom, and being the type of the infinitely understanding psycho-analyst. While Hercules, the stoical hero, freed men from the evils which threatened their lives, from the monsters which destroyed the body, Epicurus released them from the deeper and more confused terror which has its source in the religious experiences which poison life with the fear of the judgement and punishment of the avenging gods. Hercules delivered men from fear, but Epicurus freed them from anxiety. Just as Epicurus would release men from the fear of the gods, so the

[2]*De natura rerum*, III, 985 ff.

human sciences of today can redeem us from this 'sin of existence', this 'predestined guilt', which is the extreme form of inner guilt. The combination of the personalists of Christian inspiration who increasingly recall the true ethic of concrete charity; of Marxists who would so transform society that the law of love might effectively rule; and of psycho-analysts, thanks to whom the mytho-morality of 'sin' can be understood and destroyed, allows us to construct the ethic of tomorrow which is no more and no less than the true morality of Christ. Such an ethic, writes Hesnard, which is 'concrete because stripped of its mythic elements, is a morality with neither demon nor taboo; it is without the hopelessness of fate or any superstition concerning destiny; it is to be the joyous and fruitful morality which Christianity has dreamed of, but never achieved—the deed accomplished and not merely imagined, both with and for other men'.

We have examined Dr Hesnard's theory fairly thoroughly; its strengths and weaknesses should be apparent. Nonetheless it may be worth while to place the theory in its context, and thus show more exactly its good points and its usefulness for the Christian. Finally, we must try to uncover the source of the uneasiness which we experience on reading it.

In the first place it should be clear that to place

the theory within a religious context would be to show a conspicuous lack of understanding. Hesnard repeatedly claims that his book is written 'not by a moralist but by a psycho-analyst with no ideological drum to beat', and further that he makes 'no appeal to any philosophic or religious doctrine whatsoever'. He denounces sin, in the sense of inner guilt, as an illusion, 'thus limiting the meaning of the term for present purposes', and by no means denying that it can have other and equally valid meanings. His intention is not 'to call in question in any way the principles of religious and especially Christian ethics'. Nor are these mere polite expressions. There is no doubt that for Hesnard the true morality is that of the Gospel. His whole aim is in one sense to use psycho-analysis not in order to perfect or to give foundation to this morality, but in order to liberate men from the psychic malformation which prevents them from practising it to the full. True enough some of his assertions are difficult to reconcile with this intention. But the lack of precision, the ambivalence and the error of certain philosophic-sounding statements, the brevity of the somewhat simplistic cultural history of sin, are of little importance, for criticism does not always lose its force when shown to be mistaken about details. For instance, Hesnard is certainly mistaken in his interpretation of the ethic of the Old

Testament. If it is true that God alone plumbs the sinews and the heart, it is not in order to trouble the deepest intimacy of man and avenge himself on him. On the contrary he ceaselessly opens the way for the overthrow of egoism and for the entrance of that humility without which no man is open to another. 'One thing is worse than vice,' wrote Augustine, 'and that is pride in virtue.' The Old Testament inveighs against this pride because it is the worst of sins, the radical evil which shuts a man away from others. In the realm of transgression the relation of man to God in the Judeo-Christian tradition is not that of accused before his Accuser, but rather that of the one questioned before his Questioner. God is he who questions my egoism, and forces me to uproot it by showing me the chasm between the infinity of love and the finite nature of my own acts. A disgust with self can slip in unnoticed, and Hesnard is right to unmask an ever-present temptation. Every consideration of the basic motivation of one's acts can be the occasion of falling into a morbid and infantile sense of guilt. He shows correctly how this hatred of self can easily deviate into a kind of self-gratification. 'He who scorns himself, prides himself as a scorner,' wrote Nietzsche. But humility is not humiliation. Humility is in pursuit of the truth, not of hatred. The humble man is he who knows his true situation.

As St Benedict wisely remarked, 'humility is the truth of our relationship with God, a truth recognized by the intellect and accomplished by the will.'

It would be possible to examine and correct many of Dr Hesnard's interpretations, but the corrections would not be contradictions as they would follow the same general lines. Some historical and philosophical errors would be revealed as well as the occasional misinterpretation of a given moral attitude. But all this would not affect his thesis substantially, or excuse the deviations which he rightly denounces, or resolve the real problems which he poses. It is often true that the moral universe of the normal good man, and even of the Christian of today, is morbid. *Morale sans Péché* is 'a pitiless exposure of guilt'. On reading Hesnard one becomes more and more convinced of the sad fact that the modern Christian is often afraid of action. By putting the responsibility on being rather than on doing, he may easily reach the point of wishing to put an end to sin without actually doing anything. He may come to measure the state of his moral values with reference to the pain he feels in the face of evil rather than with reference to what he does about evil. Peguy has inveighed against those Christians for whom prayer had become a mystique, because it had been made into a substitute for action. It is true also that a vague bad conscience, an obscure and illusory pre-culpability is the principal source of morbid self-accusation. In fact, often the best way of curing many morbid impulses is to strip them of all moral reference, as is the case with certain forms of masturbation. There is a kind of religious education which tends to develop fear, terror and anxiety. Lucretius was not entirely mistaken. Our need of others is such that we turn in on ourselves only at the risk of hating both others and ourselves. Almost inevitably frustration becomes accusation. (Personally I see here the source of that aggressiveness of both left- and right-wing factions which vitiates the atmosphere of French Catholicism.) Mental and bodily hygiene is often a more efficacious counter to these aberrations than are moral precepts. An unknown reader wrote to me about what I had written somewhere about pleasure, happiness and joy: 'All you say of joy could be the communist's profession of his faith'. This phrase which struck me at the time came back when I was reading Hesnard. For he shows quite rightly that some joy of living is a necessary condition of morality and strikes out against sadness, as Descartes had done before him. Cartesianism is a philosophy of the happy man. Descartes wrote to the Swedish Princess Elizabeth, that 'interior joy has some secret power to turn fortune in our favour'. And

Kant, who all too often is looked on as a morose moralist, linked joy and action when he wrote: 'The joy of living comes more from the free use of life than from the object which gives us joy'. We must beware of leaving to the Marxists the sole ownership of this 'contentment' which springs from the healthy exercise of the mind. It is precisely here that Hesnard calls for a revolution in pedagogy. All education centred not on the acceptance but on the refusal of self, that is on guilt, is morbid. Nor should great stress be laid on regret and remorse, which are aspects of an unhappy and divided conscience. These feelings, however, are to be distinguished from true repentance which unites. We have just contrasted humility and humiliation, but to avoid misunderstanding we must be most explicit. God is he who questions. Ceaselessly he puts our insufficiency in question; before him there is no place for complacency. But the resulting disquiet has none of the characteristics of morbid anxiety. Every human act is finite, but this does not imply sinfulness. There is a kind of effort which is no more than impatience with limitations; and evil is in Pride or Power not in finitude. Further we must distinguish between self-accusation and self-questioning, although it is easy enough to pass from questioning to cross-examining which can degenerate into accusation. This can and should be avoided, for to suppose that there is evil at the base of everything is to misinterpret original sin. For original sin though it may be original is not originating. The Catholic Church holds that human acts can be good and meritorious. We must reaffirm our basic faith in the great enterprises of men: in work which transforms the world, in science which understands the world, and in philosophy which reflects on both work and science. Pleasure itself demands a generosity which is beyond the capacity of some; or more precisely, it demands a generosity which many force themselves to destroy. It is in one and the same act that we love ourselves, others and God.

Still, without attempting to withdraw anything of what has been said, there remains a certain uneasiness and ambiguity, stemming less from what Dr Hesnard says than from what his analyses seem to imply for him. In the first place, the distinction between authentic and morbid guilt is less clear-cut than it may appear, for they may be intertwined and the second must be eradicated without uprooting the first. And this is no easy task either in theory or in practice. The principal difficulty, however, concerns 'interiority'. Sometimes one gets the impression that the opposition set up between the subjective mytho-morality of the intention and the objective valid morality of the act is somewhat artificial. What is too lightly passed over is the fact that action itself may be unrealistic, that one may act not in order to meet the other person, but to hide from oneself. Further, this opposition is impossible for a more profound reason. Action has no meaning, or at least no moral significance, unless it is taken up by the subject and willed by him; otherwise it is not truly a human act, but merely a fact; and the intention, as the word indicates, is a movement towards the object, attention to the other person. When Kant claimed that there was only one thing absolutely good, namely a good will, he did not mean a mere velleity, or even a care for interior purification, but a real act of will, which insofar as it lay within its power developed into action. Now Dr Hesnard is aware of this and he frequently opposes to the morbid fault, which we have been discussing, 'the real internal guilt which is directed outwards by the culpable intention'. The relevant distinction, then, is not between thought and action, but, within thought itself, between all forms of narcissism and the genuine intention. The question now becomes more complex, for the opposition is no longer between internal and external morality, between intention and act, but between a true and false internal culpability. As we have already admitted, the genuine often carries the fake in its trail. But we cannot rest satisfied with asserting the possibility of error. We must go on to discover in what genuine inwardness may consist. If the second step is omitted, there is grave risk of confusing the good with the bad.

Here, then, is the kernel of the question, and we must try not to play with words at this stage. In his vigorous study 'Tyrannie et Sagesse' (in *De la Tyrannie*, Gallimard, 1954), Kojève points out that the recognition of a genuine interiority implies the existence of God. 'As long as a man is alone in knowing something, he is not sure of truly knowing it.' When, therefore, the logical and consistent atheist replaces God by society or history, interiority, if it cannot be verified in social history, is forever banished to the realm of mere opinion (*doxa*). Outside history, the atheist can discover himself only by introspection—and introspection has been jettisoned. Within this context it is easy to see how the interior may be the exterior, and how anything that is not expressed, is presumed not to exist. For the Christian, however, there is a true understanding of the interior, at least insofar as the interior is known to God. The Christian is aware that he cannot reach certainty, and for this reason must beware of the meanderings of the interior life. He is not the final judge either of himself or others; and he is free inasmuch as he leaves the business of such judgement to God who 'knows the loins and the hearts of men'. Still, this is not to say that there exists for the Christian a pure and detached interiority which is sufficient unto itself. To consider that action is secondary, and that only the intimate being of a person is of value, is one of the worst errors. Man is incarnate spirit, and the act is the truth of the intention. But it is also true that the intention creates the truth of the act, for without the intention the act would be no more than a physical fact. Intention and act are two aspects of the one inseparable reality, and it is a mistake to favour one at the expense of the other. We must clarify our idea of act. It would be wrong to see in it no more than a fact susceptible of historical analysis. As every act occurs within material nature and transforms it, material nature is not only external to man but internal as well. According to Maine de Biran we are composed of an hyper-organic force which presses against the first obstacle it comes across, namely, the body considered as a movable mass. And according to Gabriel Madinier, 'all consciousness is gesture'. Nor is it pure chance that all ethical systems have considered self-mastery as the fundamental virtue, even when they have failed to offer a satisfactory account of its nature and conditions. Effort in this sense is the so-called 'primitive fact', which by splitting consciousness allows scope for reflection and at the same time separates from the empirical 'me', the hyper-organic 'I'. Spirit works on the body, and is both the means and the model of human commitment. A moral universe exists only for the being who must first turn his efforts towards himself. 'Interiority', then, is not a given, a fully fashioned 'nature', whether good or bad, but a duality which must constantly be unified, a task by which we become ourselves, an intentionality which unites the spirit and its expression. Atheism consists in repudiating every responsibility other than responsibility before history. The Christian's responsibility is twofold: that before God and that before history. His worst errors come from despising or perverting either. Sin is not before self, but before God. By identifying sin and internal guilt or culpability Dr Hesnard involves himself in a dilemma from which he never fully extricates himself. He is caught between a coherent atheism which would deny all sin, and a genuine theism which would enable him to distinguish between, on the one hand, the truly altruistic intention based on the radical repudiation of egoism by the acceptance of a will which is at the same time both wholly other and yet profoundly personal, and on the other hand, the false internal culpability which is purely psychic and not spiritual, which has itself for its object, and which, even while hating itself, never ceases to cherish itself.

And so the question of the relation between being and doing crops up once more. Doubtless there is no entity called 'person' distinct from a person's acts; the noumenon is in the phenomenon. Nonetheless, the idea that we are more responsible for what we are, than for what we do, may be interpreted favourably. Dr Hesnard's entire work is based on the contention that there is no sin of being, no fault of existence, no guilt of destiny. The first principle of all morality as of all education is that one must accept oneself. This is perhaps the most significant lesson Hesnard's book has to offer. Yet the acceptance of self is not inevitable. His morality appears too facile. One has only to accept oneself and others, help oneself and others. Under some conditions this might be true for something which acted from instinct alone; but it would be a pre-moral state. The gravest criticism one can bring against Dr Hesnard is that his view borders on 'naturalism', and even at times unwittingly professes it. It is not with what he says, but with what he implies, that we find fault. It is not at all clear that 'brotherhood is natural', or can ever become so; and the opposition between 'vital activity' and 'aggression', as if life cannot be aggressive, is at least doubtful. It is dangerous to assert that the 'norms invoked by ethics are merely another aspect of the "normality" discovered by psycho-analysts and even biologists', and to conclude from this that we should abandon sexual morality in favour of sexual normality (leaving out of account for the moment that sexual normality is an extremely elusive entity!). It is untrue that the demands of culture are no more than the prolongation of instinctive urges, for culture transforms instinct, and is not even possible until instinct has become weak enough to allow for the working of intelligence. In a word, it is not a self-evident proposition that morality flows from the natural movement of life. These formulae, if they amounted to a coherent system, would indicate monism, while morality is essentially dualistic. The categorical imperative does not express the whole of morality, but duty can be dispensed with only by dispensing with morality as a whole. Renouvier in essentially Kantian words wrote: 'Man is an animal with precepts'. And it is on account of human animality that precepts exist. From the day when men began to exist, that is from the time when reason was opposed to sense, and liberty to nature, the moral problem came into being. For there is no morality save in a being who recognizes his duality, and strives for his unity. Like every other experience, and even more than any other experience, the moral experience reveals the duality of man. If the person is to be reunited in repentance, he must begin with the obligation of duty and the self-condemnation of remorse. Disharmony among men has its origin in the interior disharmony, which is man himself.

There are three levels of moral experience: the level of duty, the level of value, and the level of freedom and love. It is the last and highest level, freedom and love, which is morality itself. But it is not possible except insofar as it emerges from the others, and becomes incarnate in them. The true and difficult moral task is to build up humanity in oneself and in others. There would be no need to build this harmony, if it were spontaneous and natural. This dichotomy is for the Christian the moral significance of original sin. Our task was not to interpret it historically, but to recall its ethical meaning. It is man's recognition of his obligation to accept himself as divided.

But it is important to remember that the Christian does not live any longer under the law of sin but under the law of love. It is the profound though uncertain grasp of this truth which makes Dr Hesnard's book so valuable. All through his work he aims at recalling this truth to those who have forgotten it. Christianity is, or should be, the end of taboo, for within Christianity guilt comes not from the transgression of the law, but because of injury done to a person. Christianity would free men from the yoke of a purely legal ethic. For to claim that the Christian lives under the law of love is to say that he has been redeemed, and that the division within can and must be surmounted, and further has been surmounted.

Basically what I have against Dr Hesnard is that he believes morality to be too easy, and that he expects too much of it. The moral sphere is difficult, and the effort for unity is always provisional and is constantly being put in question. Morality is necessary. The moral problem is set in the depths of man's nature, and to wish to go beyond it without going through it, is to risk falling below it. But I would almost dare to say that it is here that we find original sin. It is because of the intermingling of the animal and the human that man must ceaselessly pursue his efforts for self-mastery. Because the moral sphere is the sphere of this division and of the effort to overcome it, it is also the sphere of failure and difficulty. The moral conscience risks falling into despair and anguish, if the religious conscience does not teach it that there is a place for reunification and reconciliation, and that the reign of love is possible. It is likewise true that only in this perspective of love can sin be understood in its full dramatic character. Yet the true Christian is not distressed, if he truly grasps that the central theme of Christianity is not sin but the remission of sin.

## 3

# *Traditionalism and Rationalism*

If we are to understand the problems, both religious and political, as well as the thought and behaviour of a section of the French right-wing today, we must examine the heritage of traditionalism. Auguste Comte in his pompous but precise manner, remarked: 'The immortal school which grew up at the beginning of the nineteenth century has too often been ignored. De Maistre and de Bonald were its founders, and a powerful influence in its favour was the poetry of Chateaubriand.' Lamennais, whose influence was great at a later date, is omitted, but for various reasons he did not interest Comte. But as a matter of fact this school has not been allowed to sink into oblivion. Its origins were theological, but its deepest motivations and its consequences were also political. Furthermore, it was not confined to believing Christians although it is with 'Catholic' traditionalism that we have to deal in this essay. Its alliance with positivism enabled it to exert its influence on Le Play, Taine, Renan, Brunetière, Barrès, Mauras, and the movement named Action

Française. Its theories have filtered into every branch of Catholic thought, and can be found even at the heart of movements like social Catholicism and Christian democracy, which seem diametrically opposed to it.[1] Inversely, the influence of anti-Catholic freethinking is a function of the identification of Catholicism and traditionalism. Fr de Lubac, in his study of Proudhon, shows how opposition to religion runs parallel to the growth of the authoritarian concept of theology as instanced by the *Dictionnaire de Théologie* (published by the Abbé Bergier at the close of the eighteenth century, and frequently re-edited for use in seminaries) and also to the rise of the philosophical system of Louis de Bonald and Joseph de Maistre, which was ably propagated by the early Lamennais. Renouvier is an example of someone who left the Catholic Church because he thought of it as essentially and uniquely authoritarian. In the dialogues which appeared between 1878 and 1882 in his review *Critique Religieuse*, the Catholic character defends a theory of the relation between religion and reason, which is that of Joseph de Maistre. Indeed, to understand certain fairly prevalent conceptions of authority and therefore of obedience, of truth and consequently of reason

[1]Cf. Joseph Hours, 'La doctrine de la démocratie chrétienne', *Libéralisme — Traditionalisme — Décentralisation — Cahiers de la Fondation Nationale des Sciences Politiques*, no. 31, 1952.

and conscience, of society and consequently of power and liberty, some grasp of the nature and influence of traditionalism is essential.

Louis Foucher has undertaken this study in his excellent work on Catholic philosophy in the nineteenth century.[2] We shall use this book as our source, although the author's intention was not the same as ours. He shows how traditionalism paradoxically prepared the way for the encyclical *Aeterni Patris* and for the reawakening of Thomism at the end of the century. This is an interesting historical point and Foucher's study is well done; but it is not our concern. We would discover in the historical analyses some explanation of the contemporary situation. Foucher throws light mainly on the influence of the early Lamennais and the *Essai sur l'Indifférence* ; and he shows that this influence did not cease when Lamennais left the Church. At the time many were angry with Lamennais for having, as they considered, contradicted himself; but in fact it is likely that he never contradicted himself, but merely pushed his original line of thought further in the same direction. While still young and unknown, in his *Réflexions sur l'Église de France* he praises de Bonald lavishly: 'The author of the *Législation Primitive* has discovered in these days of darkness and disorder the

[2]Cf. Louis Foucher, *La Philosophie Catholique en France au XIXième siècle avant la Renaissance thomiste et dans son rapport avec elle*, Paris 1955

last remaining hope of nations and society'. In the second volume of the *Essai*, when developing his theory of knowledge, he borrows unashamedly from de Bonald, and sets up that writer's theory as a first principle opposed to the primacy of the individual intelligence. What all men believe to be true is true. The criterion of truth is not the evidence of the proposition which announces it, but the authority of the common or general reason which accepts it. And the content of this common reason is nothing else than the primitive revelation. All knowledge among every people, whether before or after Christ, has its source not in the mind of the individual, but in the revelation made to men in the person of our first parents. The later Lamennais is implied in the earlier. The universality of the primitive revelation makes the Christian revelation redundant. Humanity and the true Church were identical. At all events the fundamental thesis remained constant. 'Believe what the human race believes.' 'Different peoples may have false prejudices,' wrote de Bonald, 'but the entire human race can have nothing but true prejudices.'

This influence was dominant through practically all French Catholic life and thought for nearly a century. In 1825 Augustin Bonnetty, then twenty-five years of age, found in the *Essai* the definitive orientation of his thought, and he was able to continue until 1855 as the editor of two journals with Lamennaisian leanings without ever being troubled by the Catholic authorities. Both Lacordaire, who was at first entirely won over to traditionalism, and Gerbet continued to teach a 'moderate traditionalism' even after the condemnation of Lamennais. Beyond the confines of professional philosophy the Chesnaie group remained faithful to the general orientation of the *Essai*, and even pushed it further in the authoritarian direction. Rohrbacher, Guéranger and Combalot contributed to its triumph in Church history, liturgy and preaching. Abbé Maret makes use of Lamennais' brand of traditionalism to criticize eclecticism. This anti-rationalist tendency was reinforced by the growth of another movement in Catholic thinking, the 'fideism' of Abbé Bautain. In 1852 the Jesuit Chastel in his *The Church and Modern Philosophical Systems* pointed out the continued vigour of Lamennaisian traditionalism, and proved his point with apt citations from contemporary Catholic writings. It was given a new impetus as a result of the political and social upheavals following the 1848 Revolution. Its social principles were given currency by such periodicals as Veuillot's *Univers* and the influential *Monde Catholique*. Thus traditionalism remained vigorous despite continued warnings from Rome, buoyed up by its conviction that it enshrined the true and integral spirit of Catholicism. This then is the source if not of integrism itself, at least of Catholic integralism, which is all the more widespread as it corresponds to a deeply-felt conviction, namely, the call to unity.

De Maistre and de Bonald did no more than cast into systematic form a common sentiment, which was already fairly powerful before the Revolution of 1789, and which was essentially a reaction against the dry-as-dust philosophy of the Enlightenment. So it is not altogether surprising that Rousseau could be thought of as the founder of traditionalism. He is frequently quoted by the traditionalists; and de Bonald discovered in his writings the basis for his own theory of the divine origin of language. Comte was right in saying that the 'poetic alliance' of Chateaubriand gave to the dawn of the nineteenth century and to traditionalism all its power to captivate public opinion. Between the mentality of the turn of the century around the year 1800 and traditionalism there was a natural harmony. Traditionalism began as opposition, and did not come into its own until it was firmly established as the counter-revolution. The origin of the Revolution seemed to have been Cartesian rationalism and the Encyclopedia which followed from it. According to Lamennais the rationalist attitude characteristic of the eighteenth century stems from the application of the Cartesian method of the quest for evidence and the systematic doubt in the individual mind. The first step in the traditionalist counter-revolution is quite naturally an attack on reason and philosophy. 'The French Revolution was fought under the standard of philosophy,' wrote Cournot, 'and so nothing was more natural to the counter-revolution than to attack philosophy, and thus indirectly undermine the Revolution itself.' Rather than supplant one philosophy by another the aim was to overthrow philosophy as such. For philosophy, inasmuch as it is an autonomous rational pursuit, was considered the source of all evil. The fundamental error was to seek personal evidence instead of submitting to the authority either of nature or nature's child, society. The authority of evidence yielded to the evidence of authority. The greatest and seminal virtue was humility in the sense of submission: submission to facts, submission to power, submission to the Church, and always submission to tradition. As was to be expected, de Bonald pushed the idea to the extreme: 'Men should not be assembled save in the Church or the army, for there they do not think, but only listen and obey'. It is this attitude which is the unique source of the different traditionalist schools and of their common hatred for thought. For the great philosophers reason was a common ground. When a Christian and a Chinese philosopher understand a theorem in geometry they are united in and by intelligence. For the traditionalists, intelligence isolates, divides, separates. To think is dangerous, for it leads to opposition and division. The greatest risk is to think for oneself instead of living like everyone else. Perhaps it is here at its very source that we should find its basic flaw. Instead of being the natural sequel of the old France, it was merely the denial of the new; instead of being authentically traditional, it was artificially reactionary; instead of calling for a renewal, it demanded a restoration.

This reaction against the France of the Revolution was common to the whole of Europe; and it was one of the original blemishes of the traditionalist movement, that it was as little French as possible, and relied too much on foreign influence. Its two founders, de Maistre and de Bonald, were either not French at all (de Bonald came from Savoy) or had emigrated from France (de Maistre had been influenced by German thought during his time in Heidelberg). Lamennais himself was a Breton with the mystic's sense of the divine and of the communion of all men. He had a love for Ireland with which he felt some community of spirit; for a Polish virgin martyr; for Rhineland Germany whose romantic movement he admired; and above all for the Middle Ages as seen through the eyes of Chateaubriand. The traditionalists were united by two things: defiance of the contemporary French state, and ultramontanism so brilliantly defended by de Maistre in *Du Pape*. Traditionalism and romanticism are inextricably linked together. 'The original romanticism,' wrote Renouvier, 'because it freed men from the eighteenth century, at first favoured the authoritarian movement.' Maurras' polemics have popularized many false notions, and traditionalism is often imagined to have been a new classicism, heir of eighteenth-century France and sworn enemy of all romanticism. As a matter of fact it was born of romanticism, and far from continuing the classical tradition it opposed it. Against the classical tradition it set a legendary and romantic version of the Middle Ages. Romanticism, especially the German variety, is an exaltation of the deep spiritual life against the superficiality of reason and intelligence. Traditionalism and romanticism are united in their common hatred for everything which was tainted with 'intellect'. What is lived in community, is set against what is thought in solitude. As Julien Benda wittily remarked, the ultimate and underlying argument of the traditionalists runs: 'Do you realize that you are thinking differently from me?'

The organicism and vitalism which can be found in romanticism, are equally constituents of traditionalism. These have given to certain sections of the right wing, not the 'pluralism' which Simone de Beauvoir thinks one of its chief marks, but the worst kind of unitarism. The traditionalists to a man defend a total unity in every sphere whether religious, political, economic or social. And this unity is always intensely felt and lived. To such an extent is this true that de Maistre, although he recognized in pantheism one of the greatest of the dangers besetting his time, could not help but consider it as an unfortunate deviation from the great idea of unity.[3] Society itself was a kind of pyramid, a hierarchical unit, an organism subject to natural laws which would inevitably punish the law-breaker. This is the source of confidence in pure experience unsystematized by intelligence. Traditionalism can be expressed in a three-fold dichotomy: experience against intelligence, society against the individual, order against progress. For example we may take the common mythology of medicine. The traditionalists would be the doctors

[3]'Our present unity results from our basic unity in God. Malebranche's theory that we see everything in God, is no more than a superb commentary on the Pauline"In him we move and have our being". The pantheism of the Stoics and Spinoza is a corruption of this great ideal; but always there is the same principle, the same tendency towards unity' (Joseph de Maistre). This unity towards which men aspire as to their supreme good, but which they cannot reach of their own efforts, has been revealed. It is Catholicism. Catholicism is then the only religion which answers the need common to all men, and which fulfils their aspirations. It is the unity by which all diversity is explained. Outside it there is but division and error. It is the master-key to knowledge, for without it nothing can be known. This is the ultimate reason why everything must depend not on unassisted intelligence which cannot by itself reach the final unity by which all is explained, but on intelligence illuminated by faith. Cf. Jean Lacroix, *Vocation personnelle et Tradition nationale*.

of society. On the naïve view, such as Carrel's,[4] the doctor is unavoidably an organicist. Even Gustave Thibon thought that if biological analogies were always deficient, at least 'they are the best available, and it is certain that the medical profession, if the doctor puts his soul into his work, is the surest road to political wisdom'. De Maistre's contrast between the living word, which was the expression of the whole person, body and soul, and the dead written word emerging from cold and prejudiced reason, is in the same spirit. 'You cannot write in men's souls with a pen.' Only what is handed down orally through generations, what adapts to nature and society, what is transformed without need of definition, is of worth. The exaltation of custom springs from this notion. The written constitution is a violation of all that is natural and organic in society. The choice is between destructive reason and living tradition.

The constant theme is anti-rationalism, the impotence of reason. It is significant that in the nineteenth century the terms 'primitivism' and 'traditionalism' were interchangeable. For they gave pride of place to what was primitive in man, instinct, nature, life, as opposed to the superstructure of reason. The older, and more primitive

[4]Cf. F. Dagognet, *Philosophie Biologique*, Paris 1955, in which a case is made for the viability of what the author calls, paradoxically enough, non-experimental medicine.

was considered true, because it had endured. But 'primitive' refers also to the set of common beliefs on which the universal society of the whole human race was thought to be founded. This set of beliefs was a true general legislation, which was contained in the original revelation and which is handed down from generation to generation. The individual never has the right to question the collective and universal reason because of doubts in his individual mind. For he owes his reason to society which has transmitted to him its knowledge, the means of each of his intellectual operations. These two meanings of 'primitive' have a common source in a profounder meaning on which de Bonald insists in his *Législation Primitive*. There is but one source of knowledge and the essential revelation, more important than the Mosaic or even than the Christian, is the primitive revelation made to our first parents. In it all the possible objects of thought are revealed, and reason by itself discovers nothing. If the ancient philosophers, Chinese, Greek or Roman, held and taught some truths, this was not because they had discovered them by the power of their own thought. Rather was it that the memory of the original revelation, first given to Adam and since transmitted to all humanity, had come to fruition in them. De Bonald did not agree with Lamennais on all points; but he congratulated him for having shown that 'the greatest and most worth-while philosophy consists in submitting reason to the truth of religion'. Reason by itself is worthless, or more exactly its worth is secondary, limited and derived. According to their well-known dictum human reason demonstrates but does not inquire, that is, it can organize already acquired truths, but it cannot discover them for itself. In his review of *Législation Primitive* Chateaubriand wrote that the power of reasoning was entirely dependent on the primitive truths; philosophy must no longer be thought of as the search for truth; it must be content to be a wisdom of life. For Hegel philosophy is the truth of religion; for the traditionalists, religion was the truth of philosophy. Even Lacordaire in 1832, and Gerbet after his Roman period in 1838, both maintained the central authoritarian theses which excluded the search for truth from the scope of reason. Basically, traditionalism amounts to maintaining authoritarianism in theology, and therefore the radical heteronomy of philosophy. It should not be forgotten that Maine de Biran whose political theories resembled those of de Bonald, but who was the more critical of the two, entitled his criticism of traditionalism a *Defence of Philosophy*, and of the human person.

If authoritarianism was able to impose itself on the theology of the Church in France for almost a century without encountering any opposition other than an ontologism which was equally condemned by Rome, the reason for this is that in the spheres of politics, economics and sociology the Church in France seemed to be in agreement with authoritarianism. De Bonald in 1820 claimed that his work had been to show the 'close unity between political and religious truths'. And Bonnetty, the staunch advocate of Lamennais' brand of traditionalism, wrote that, 'we are coming to understand that the whole of religion rests on tradition, that is on history rather than on reasoning'. This school began a type of apologetics which defends religion because of its external effects; it shows for instance that religion is the natural support of political, economic and social stability. This was followed later by what may be termed 'externalist apologetics', whose champions, though not themselves Christians, tried to show the truth of Catholicism by its agreement with the social nature of man. Joseph de Maistre pushed this attitude to the extreme when he wrote that even superstition must be defended as an 'outpost of religion'. In its most moderate form traditionalism recognized three authorities: the authority of facts which impose themselves in the sciences and which are the very words of God (science therefore is worthless except insofar as it is rooted in religion); the authority of the temporal power, of society, for the sake of moral and political truths, which philosophy is powerless to discover, but which are contained in the primitive revelation, and are handed on by tradition; and finally the authority of the spiritual power, of the Church, in all things concerning the Christian faith. It is typical of Lamennais to call beliefs certitudes of fact in order to distinguish them from the rational certitudes reached by demonstration; even in revelation experience is set against reason. Distorting the views of Malebranche to suit his ends, de Bonald makes a distinction between knowledge by reason which yields personal opinion, and knowledge by instinctive feeling which is collective. Experience is the criterion of reality. Domestic, patriotic and religious sentiments attach us to our families, our country and our Church. To feel with something is to be attached to it, to be incapable of doubting it, to be one with it. So belief in God is not by proof but by universal experience, that is, consent in its etymological sense of 'feeling with'. Opinion divides, sentiment unites. The traditionalists love whatever seems to them natural and organic. Inasmuch as he is an individual, man is evil and corrupt; as a social being he is redeemed and good. 'We are bad by nature, but good by society' (de Bonald). Traditionalists are organic rather than authoritarian, for authority is but the keystone of a naturally hierarchic society.

The origin of this generalized authoritarianism

must be sought in their theory of belief. The basic theorem is that belief must always precede doubt. If the belief comes from outside, there is no need to doubt it, or to examine its evidence, but to admit it according to purely external criteria. Doubt is anti-social. Nature is not disturbed if a man doubts, but society is disturbed. One must begin by saying, I believe. Other philosophers, Lavelle for instance, may think of the act of faith as consubstantial with spirit; spirit is that which before any proof has faith in itself. But this is not the traditionalist position. It is not a matter of spirit's fundamental confidence in itself, but rather a first and definitive submission to some external authority. What is imposed is a spontaneous and immediate belief transmitted by society. It is natural that man should be taught. It is clear that belief defined in this manner is identical with authority. Only this is essential. Sometimes, though rarely, and then more often in Germany than in France, this attitude can be accompanied with 'leftist' political leanings. De Bonald himself defended positions approaching state socialism. The State is responsible for all the families which compose it, and must take care of those unable to fend for themselves. There is a kind of Christian socialism not incompatible with traditionalism. The one thing which is totally unacceptable is the effort to think or judge for oneself. 'The clergy must be opposed, for they may be socialist but never liberal.' This is not true of all the clergy, but it could be said with truth of the traditionalists. This is the mentality which we have referred to as 'Catholic integralism'. It consists mainly in being an integralist in the religious sphere, and in being a 'progressive' in the political and social sphere. By social progress was meant progress inspired directly by Catholicism and worked out within the context of Christian customs and institutions. In short, anything could be accepted if only the authoritarian principle was saved.

From the beginning of the nineteenth century, and especially perhaps after 1848, Catholic and even non-Catholic opinion was 'passionately attached to the idea of authority, unity, permanence and antiquity in intellectual matters'. As Henri Guillemin has shown, the rift between the Church and the working class can be dated from the years 1848 to 1852. The ever-present influence of traditionalism, even among its supposed adversaries, is a partial explanation of this. In *Univers* Montalembert wrote of the December plebiscite (1851): 'I have made my choice. I am for authority against revolt; for conservation against destruction; for society against socialism'. Quite early Rome came out against traditionalism. In 1834 the encyclical *Singulari Vos* condemned the 'erroneous philosophical system of recent origin' (Lamennais'

*Essai*) which, 'in place of the holy and apostolic traditions which are the foundation of Christian teaching, has substituted vague, uncertain, and futile doctrines'. Still, for a long period these condemnations had no practical effect. The excesses of traditionalism were condemned, but a 'moderate traditionalism' was permitted and even encouraged. The doctrine was clear, but there was some diplomatic reluctance to condemn out of hand a system and movement which supported Rome's own ultramontane claims. 'In the eyes of the Church,' wrote Louis Foucher, 'the teachings of de Bonald, de Maistre and the early Lamennais seemed to be a healthy break from the anti-Christian rationalism widespread in France and elsewhere in Europe during the eighteenth century. From this point of view the Church's intellectual authorities were favourably disposed toward it. It might be said that the Church thought she might be able to accept traditionalism insofar as it could be adapted into her own philosophical tradition.'

Nothing reveals better the influence and mentality of traditionalism than its polemic against eclecticism. Émile Bréhier in his *Histoire de la Philosophie* mentions the need for a study of this aspect of the subject, which M. Foucher has now undertaken with success. Its philosophical interest may be slight, but it shows a characteristic spirit.

In the first place Victor Cousin's replies to the attacks are a valuable key to the atmosphere of the time. To the traditionalists who accused him of pantheism, he replied that it was the Church which had lost her genuine traditions and fundamental rationalism. In the nineteenth century, he went on, there came a man who broke away from the genuine tradition of the Church, and would admit but one principle, authority. True, Lamennais was no more. But 'his doctrine has infiltrated the clergy; and the Church in France in the persons of its young men has been dealt a fatal blow. The Church has rejected Lamennais; but although his system is not retained, the spirit which animated him is not dead'. Traditionalism brought momentary glory to the Church; but that glory was soon tarnished, and even today its 'bad influence remains, contrary to the national traditions of the Church, contrary to its abiding interests, to the declarations of the Councils, and to the eternal spirit of Catholicism'. The fiercest episode in the dispute between Cousin and the traditionalists was occasioned by Cousin's new philosophical course of lectures completed in 1832. This unleashed a most violent attack upon the author, which lasted until his retirement under the Second Empire more than twenty years later. Yet there is nothing subversive in the lectures. They are openly spiritualist, affirm the independence of the soul and its survival after death, as well as the existence of a personal God whom men are bound to adore. But from the traditionalist point of view the stumbling block is here. De Bonald in one of his thought-provoking aphorisms puts his finger on the crucial point. To prove God's existence is to strip faith of all worth. In his *Essai sur le Panthéisme dans les Sociétés Modernes* (1839) Abbé Maret, and here the whole traditionalist movement was squarely behind him, came out strongly against any attempt to speak of God on the philosophical level, and against any conception of the human intelligence as 'inquisitive'. Cousin's new course of lectures, by separating reason and faith (which his earlier course of 1823 had not done) seemed an intolerable encroachment on the preserve of Christian theology.

In this context we can better understand the importance and exact significance of the Vatican Council's declaration that the human intelligence can reach God by natural means. To deny that reason can reach a knowledge of God, is to strip reason of all its ontological capacity and reduce it to the level of the phenomenal. By upholding the ontological capacity of reason the Vatican Council re-established, against the most basic tenet of traditionalism, the genuine Christian tradition of *capax entis, capax Dei*.

The damage done by traditionalism can scarcely be exaggerated. In the first place it alienated non-

Catholics, for its apologetics produced confusion on both the intellectual and social plane, and on the question of Catholicism and authority. For many non-Catholics, not least among whom were Proudhon and Renouvier, the defence of man, of the individual, of science and philosophy, of reason itself went hand in hand with an attack on Catholicism which they identified with traditionalism. The traditionalists favoured this identification. Convinced of their integral Catholicity, they identified themselves with Christianity, and claimed theirs to be the sole Christian philosophy. Mgr Hugonin wrote in 1856 of the danger of such identification, and spoke against the misuse of the terms 'Catholic' and 'Christian'. The following quotation is from his *Ontologie:* 'The modern rationalist school, which has among its members some fine philosophers and writers, was formed at the time when the disciples of Lamennais were preaching their reform, and were setting themselves up as the representatives of Christianity; their philosophy affected the name "Christian philosophy", by which they meant that those who refused to accept their principles ceased to belong to the religion of Jesus Christ. The new generation of intellectuals, who were ignorant enough of the dogmas of our faith, were introduced to them solely through the books and periodicals of the reformers. Thus they came to regard Christianity as the sworn enemy of all speculation and of all science save the tabulation of facts'.

In the second place the effects of traditionalism among believers were no less disastrous, and they are far from having entirely disappeared. Intelligence and reason cannot be disparaged with impunity, for they are the structure of intellectual and moral conscience. The influence of traditionalism goes hand in hand with the decline of conscience which is denounced as individual, 'Protestant' and merely subjective. Here too the true Christian tradition is thwarted. For the true tradition is that one must educate and inform one's conscience, but must never act against it.[5] The habit of surrendering one's own responsibility into the hands of an exterior authority, of being unable to find security save in extrinsic obedience and submission, leads to the worst deformation of the human person. And such attitudes and modes of behaviour can remain long after the doctrines, which were

[5]Laberthonnière, whose writings were often polemical and rebellious, but whose life was a wonderful example of obedience and freedom combined, wrote in his *La Notion Chrétienne de l'Authorité* (Paris 1955 160–1): 'It is foolish to try to belittle or ignore conscience under the pretext of rooting out subjectivism. For conscience will remain despite your efforts, and will make itself heard. But there is no better way of stifling its voice than by submitting it to an absolute authoritarianism. For it is the lesson of history that there have never been worse subjectivists—to use the fashionable term—than those who began by wishing to admit nothing but authority, and by declaring that they submitted to nothing but what was objective.'

their source, have been rejected. Louis Foucher does not go into such questions as these. His aim was purely to write a scientific history of the period. But in throwing light on this epoch in the intellectual history of the Church in France, he prompts us to some healthy reflections. For better or for worse, what has been slowly built up over a period of time, is not pulled down in a day; what one age produces, another must perfect, or reform.